MW01103511

SEXUALLY TRANSMITTED DISEASES

—Diseases and People—

SEXUALLY TRANSMITTED DISEASES

Christine Perdan Curran

Enslow Publishers, Inc.

44 Fadem Road   PO Box 38
Box 699   Aldershot
Springfield, NJ 07081   Hants GU12 6BP
USA   UK

Library of Congress Cataloging-in-Publication Data

Curran, Christine Perdan.
    Sexually transmitted diseases / Christine Perdan Curran.
        p. cm. — (Diseases and people)
    Includes bibliographical references and index.
    Summary: Examines the history, symptoms, treatment, and prevention of such
sexually transmitted diseases as syphilis, gonorrhea, herpes, AIDS, and hepatitis.
    ISBN 0-7660-1050-3
    1. Sexually transmitted diseases—Juvenile literature. [1. Sexually transmitted
diseases.] I. Title. II. Series.
    RC200.2.C86   1998
    616.95' 1—dc21   97-44140
                                                CIP
                                                AC

Printed in the United States of America

10 9 8 7 6 5 4 3 2 1

Illustration Credits: BioStar, Inc., p. 92; Colleen Kelley, pp. 27, 29, 30, 39, 42,
54, 71, 75, 79, 97; Marty Plumbo, University of Cincinnati, pp. 13, 47, 59; Bruce
M. Rothschild, Director, Arthritis Center of Northeast Ohio, Youngstown, Ohio,
p. 16; Tuskegee University Archives, p. 66; Jim Veneman, p. 86.

Cover Illustration: Christine Perdan Curran

Contents

SEXUALLY TRANSMITTED DISEASES

What is it? Any disease that can be transmitted through sexual contact. Sexually transmitted diseases (STDs) used to be called venereal diseases. The word *venereal* comes from *Venus*, the Roman goddess of love.

Who gets it? Both sexes get STDs, although women are generally at greater risk than men. Teens are at higher risk than older adults. Newborns can catch the disease if their mothers have it.

How do you get it? STDs are transmitted by intimate sexual contact or passed from an infected mother to her newborn. Health care or emergency workers are also at risk when treating patients who are infected. Contaminated needles used for injecting drugs or creating tattoos can also spread STDs.

What are the symptoms? There are various symptoms, including sores on the genitals, unusual discharges from the penis or vagina, itching, and pain in the lower abdomen.

How are STDs treated? Bacterial and fungal infections can be treated with antibiotics. Many viral diseases are incurable. Parasites such as lice are treated with pesticides.

How can they be prevented? Avoiding all sexual contact and contact with the blood or other bodily fluids of an infected person, and using a condom during sexual activity prevents STDs.

1

A Complicated Problem

André tried using ointment. He tried using aloe. He even tried an over-the-counter antibiotic cream. But the sore was still there.

"It kind of looks like a . . . cut or scrape . . . and I like just wanted it to go away."[1]

André knew about sexually transmitted diseases (STDs). At the age of twenty-seven, he had already been treated more than once for gonorrhea, a bacterial STD. However, he also thought he finally knew how to tell if a woman was "safe." His sexual partner looked healthy. She looked "clean." He was sure she could not have been responsible for the raw, red spot on his penis.[2]

André now knows a little more than he did before about sexually transmitted diseases. He knows that a healthy appearance can fool a person. He knows that home remedies and over-the-counter medicines are not strong enough to cure these diseases. And he knows that the doctors and nurses who work in sexually transmitted disease clinics are there to help, not to scold.

It took a single shot of penicillin to cure André of his sexually transmitted disease. It turned out the sore was the first symptom of a syphilis infection, another bacterial STD. Since André had had sex with more than one woman, health care workers tried hard to track down anyone who might have been infected with syphilis. They were not able to find all of his partners.[3] There are many people like André in the world. When you cannot treat all the victims, the diseases spread.

Each year, there are about 12 million new cases of sexually transmitted diseases in the United States. Three million of those cases involve teenagers.[4] Worldwide, the numbers are shocking. There were more than 333 million cases in 1995, and the number of new cases increases every year.[5]

The health risks of sexually transmitted diseases are enormous. AIDS and hepatitis B are killers. Syphilis and gonorrhea can have horrifying effects on babies born to women with the diseases. Other diseases can hide their effects for years, eventually leading to cancer or infertility. In addition, being infected with some sexually transmitted diseases makes it easier to become infected with HIV, the virus that causes AIDS.

The economic costs are also high. In the United States, the major STDs are a $10 billion burden on the economy. When you add in the impact of AIDS cases caused by sexual contact, the cost jumps to $17 billion.[6] However, very little of that money is being spent to study or prevent the diseases. Most of the money is spent treating people to cure their infections or treating the complications that can result from STDs. Since many sexually transmitted diseases can never be cured, treatment often lasts for years.

There are more than twenty different diseases that can be transmitted, or passed from one person to another, by sexual contact. The diseases are caused by a wide range of organisms, including bacteria and viruses. A few can also be spread without sexual contact. Thus, it is no surprise so many people get infected every year.

It will take a lot of work to bring sexually transmitted diseases under control, but health workers are hopeful. They point to Canada, where syphilis has nearly disappeared, and Scandinavia, where STD rates are low despite a high rate of sexual activity.[7] The solution appears to be better education, better communication, and better medical care available to everyone, no matter where in the world they live.

2

The History of STDs

Uncovering the history of most sexually transmitted diseases is much more difficult than looking up background information on well-documented diseases such as the flu, the measles, or even the notorious Black Death (bubonic plague). The stigma or embarrassment attached to diseases transmitted through sexual contact was so great that many early medical historians did not even discuss the topic. Others included descriptions of diseases without realizing the diseases were sexually transmitted.

Syphilis

There is one sexually transmitted disease that has been well documented, however. The disease is syphilis, and its history is so controversial that people still argue about it today. When they are arguing, the name that comes up most often is the name of the famous explorer Christopher Columbus.[1]

The Niña, the Pinta, and Syphilis Too?

Many people believe that Columbus and his crew brought back much more than gold and other treasures from the New World they discovered in 1492. They believe that Columbus's ships also carried back to Europe the germ that causes syphilis, a sexually transmitted disease.[2]

There are several good reasons why people believe this. Since people living in the West Indies had already developed a treatment for the disease—an extract from the tropical guaiacum tree—they must have had a need for a treatment.[3] Scientists also found evidence of syphilis in the bones of people who lived in the Americas before Columbus ever arrived. But when scientists looked at the skeletons of people living in Asia, Africa, and Europe before Columbus's time, they did not find any evidence of the disease.[4] Another damaging piece of evidence involves the timing of the world's only syphilis epidemic. Shortly after Columbus returned to Europe, a very horrifying and deadly strain of syphilis spread across the continent.[5]

"By slow degrees the corruption, arising in the generative organs, consumes the whole body," wrote Italian physician Girolamo Fracastoro, the man who named the disease syphilis. In his 1530 book, Fracastoro provided an early account of its symptoms.[6] His description was a mixture of poetry and medical advice typical of sixteenth-century doctors who were well trained in both science and philosophy.

> Then the arms, the shoulder blades, and the calves of the legs are racked with pain. Forthwith, throughout the body unsightly scabs break forth, and foully defile the face and breast. The malady now takes a new form: a pustule resembling the top of an acorn. . . .[7]

Barcelona physician Ruy Diaz de Isla had a much simpler description for syphilis. He called it the "reptilian disease" because of the way it disfigured its victims.[8]

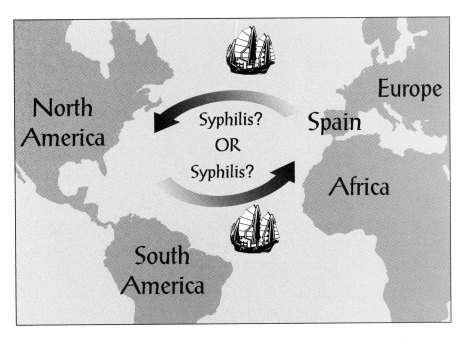

Syphilis was probably brought back to Europe from the New World, although there are other explanations for its spread around the world.

The syphilis epidemic spread throughout Europe into eastern Asia. Its route can easily be traced following the paths of the great armies that marched through Europe at the time. The army of King Charles VIII of France carried the disease into Italy during the fifteenth century. Oliver Cromwell's English troops took syphilis northward into Scotland during the seventeenth century. The Seven Years' War involved troops from many different countries from northern and central Europe. Once again, the spread of war helped to spread syphilis. Swedish troops brought the disease back home with them when the Seven Years' War ended in 1762.[9]

The Blame Is in the Name

The attempts to control the spread of syphilis in Europe went hand in hand with attempts to fix blame. As the epidemic spread from country to country, the new victims would name the disease after the culture they believed was responsible for spreading the illness.

The Italians blamed the French, calling the disease *Morbus Gallicus*, which literally means the "French disease." The French, in turn, blamed the Italians. Their nickname for syphilis was *mala Napoletana*, a reference to a major outbreak in the city of Naples following the invasion of King Charles's troops. The accusations continued across Europe. The Russians blamed the Poles. The Persians blamed the Turks. The Spanish called syphilis "Indian measles," blaming the New World natives who returned to Europe aboard Columbus's ships.[10]

Early Attempts at Control and Treatment

Although Fracastoro did not believe at first that syphilis came from the New World, he did know about the natives' homegrown cure from the tropical guaiacum tree and included a description of it in his later writings. Fracastoro believed an application of mercury ointment worked better. Mercury remained a common treatment for syphilis for the next three hundred years.[11]

Prevention became the most important tool in fighting syphilis. The military had an important role to play in this fight since many sailors and soldiers hired prostitutes, which put them in great danger of getting syphilis. The British government passed three laws to control sexually transmitted diseases. They were known as the Contagious Disease Acts, and the first one became law in 1864.[12]

Women had virtually no rights under England's Contagious Disease Acts. They could be stopped in the streets and forced to undergo medical examinations. They were locked up if they either showed symptoms of a sexually transmitted disease or refused to be examined. The restrictions were applied most harshly in the towns and ports where soldiers and sailors lived. This made the towns very popular with rich Englishmen, who wanted to be sure the prostitutes they hired were free of disease.

The laws, however, did nothing to punish the free-wheeling soldiers, sailors, and gentlemen who used prostitutes, or men who were infected with a sexually transmitted disease. "The

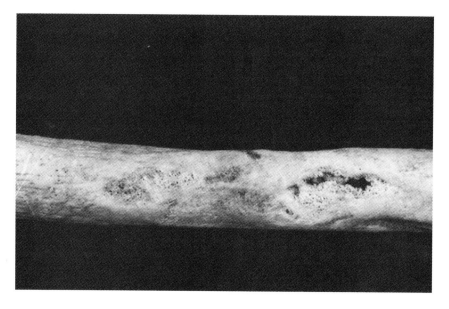

The effects of syphilis can be seen in this bone.

possibility of quarantining men who had the disease was never considered," noted sociologist Margaret Stacey.[13]

Gonorrhea: The World's First Known STD

Gonorrhea is the world's oldest known sexually transmitted disease. The ancient Egyptians described its symptoms in their writings. By the time of Hippocrates, the famous Greek doctor who lived in the fourth century B.C., most physicians realized the disease was passed from person to person through sexual contact. The disease picked up the name *gonorrhea* in the second century A.D. The name means "flow of seed," which refers to the dripping pus from the tip of the penis, one of the most noticeable symptoms of the disease.

At the time of the great syphilis epidemic of the fifteenth century, some doctors thought syphilis was just a new, more deadly form of the already existing disease gonorrhea. Others believed syphilis was a distinctly different disease. It took four centuries before scientists and doctors had the ability to distinguish syphilis and gonorrhea. The debate was settled by German skin doctor Albert Neisser in 1879. He identified the germ that causes gonorrhea and showed that the symptoms of gonorrhea were different from those of syphilis. As a result of his work, the gonorrhea bacterium, gonococcus, was named after Neisser. Its scientific name is *Neisseria gonorrhoeae*.[14]

By the time of Neisser's work, doctors also knew that gonorrhea could cause blindness in babies born to women who were infected. Because gonorrhea was so widespread, this was the most common cause of blindness in children. In 1883, German doctors began treating newborns' eyes with silver nitrate to prevent infection. That preventive medicine was very effective, but doctors still had no effective way to treat gonorrhea infections in adults.[15]

Herpes in History

Ancient Egyptian medical texts from 1550 B.C. also include the symptoms of a disease that closely match the symptoms of herpes, a viral disease that can be transmitted by sexual activity. The Egyptians wrote about sores that could be found in both the genital region and around the mouth. The name came from the ancient Greeks, and it means "to creep." The name refers to the way herpes sores can spread across the

17

body.[16] The herpesvirus was isolated and identified in 1934 by Dr. Albert Sabin. (Sabin is most famous for developing a vaccine against polio.)

Twentieth-Century Battles

By the early twentieth century, people feared syphilis in the same way that people worry about cancer and heart disease today. It was that common and that devastating. However, doctors were making important progress in understanding and fighting some sexually transmitted diseases. The syphilis bacterium was identified in 1905.[17] Scientist Paul Ehrlich and his assistant developed a new treatment for syphilis in 1909 called Salvarsan. Unfortunately, Salvarsan injections contained arsenic, which is poisonous, so the treatment was very risky. The development of antibiotics, beginning with penicillin in 1943, finally gave doctors a safe and effective treatment against the most common bacterial STDs.[18]

Medical advances did nothing to stop racist and sexist government attacks against those suffering from sexually transmitted diseases. The Nazi government in Germany used its strong police powers to enforce tough public health laws. No one infected with a sexually transmitted disease was allowed to get married. Anyone who had sex while infected could be thrown into prison for three years. The Nazis considered STDs a "degenerate disease" of drunkards and single mothers, for example.[19]

STDs in America

The American government began a public awareness program against sexually transmitted diseases in 1938 with the United States Syphilis Control Program. The government focused on syphilis, because it was the most widespread STD and had the most damaging health effects. The health workers in the program ran into problems right from the start. Most syphilis victims and their doctors would not report the illness, so it was nearly impossible to find out how many people actually had the disease. By the time penicillin came along, doctors knew they could beat the disease if they could find infected people and treat them before they infected others.[20]

The syphilis problem gained the public's attention when celebrities fell ill. Composer Scott Joplin, who wrote some of the world's most famous ragtime music, was an early American celebrity who fell victim to syphilis. The disease destroyed his body and his brain. Joplin died in a mental institution in New

Yearly Cases of Curable STDs Worldwide[21]

Trichomoniasis	170 million
Chlamydia	89 million
Gonorrhea	62 million
Syphilis	12 million

York City after battling the disease for years. He had a daughter who died shortly after birth. She, too, may have been a victim of the horrid disease.[22]

Changing Views of STDs

Social views of sexually transmitted diseases have changed over the centuries, often depending on how widespread the diseases were and how much damage they were doing. During the great European syphilis epidemic, people were terrified of the disease. Religious artists drew sketches showing the disease as divine punishment. The drawings showed evil people being struck down while the holy ones were spared.[23]

During the Renaissance, many people developed a more casual attitude toward sex and sexually transmitted diseases. Catching an STD was considered "an unavoidable little accident."[24] Emperors, kings, and other wealthy nobles were often infected, but they had better medical care and suffered fewer serious side effects, so they did not worry very much.[25]

As the world's population grew, there was much greater pressure to remain a virgin before marriage and to remain faithful to your spouse after marriage. A similar shift in attitudes was seen during the beginning of the HIV epidemic. The sexual freedoms of the 1960s and 1970s gave way to much more conservative views and a new emphasis on "family values" in the 1980s and 1990s.

Bacterial STDs

Less than 25 percent of young women believe they are at risk of getting a sexually transmitted disease. Barrie Andrews proves how wrong most young women are. She was getting ready to go to college when she contracted an infection that nearly killed her. Her doctors believe it was caused by a bacterium called chlamydia. At first, Barrie ignored her symptoms. Her menstrual periods had become irregular. Her stomach hurt. When she reported her complaints to the doctor, they were not taken seriously. Over time, the infection weakened Barrie's body and allowed other bacteria to invade. The bacteria spread through her reproductive system and caused pelvic inflammatory disease, an infection of her fallopian tubes. The complications left her unable to have children.[1]

Barrie's illness was so bad she had to spend two weeks getting antibiotics pumped directly into her blood. The bacteria fought just as hard as Barrie's doctors. The infection flared back up seven times. Finally, Barrie recovered, but she needed several operations to repair the damage caused by the germs. Today, she is better and more aware of the danger of STDs. "People don't know how common these diseases are, what symptoms to look for, and how deadly serious they can be."[2]

With more than 12 million new cases of STDs each year in the United States,[3] and with sex education classes in most schools, it might be surprising to find out that many Americans cannot name a single sexually transmitted disease.[4] There are more than twenty STDs, but only a few of these diseases are widely known. We will look at the most common STDs and the bacteria, viruses, and other germs that cause them.

Syphilis: The "Bad Blood" Disease

"Bad blood" is just one of the many nicknames for syphilis. It is an appropriate name, because blood infected by the bacteria that cause syphilis carries the bacteria throughout the body. The bacterium has a very distinctive shape. Called spirochetes, the bacteria look like tiny coils or spirals under the microscope.

Syphilis can only be spread by direct contact with infected tissues. The spirochetes are passed from person to person during sexual intercourse (vaginal or anal) or through oral sex. The bacteria are very fragile and die quickly outside the warm, moist tissues of the human body, so it is impossible to catch syphilis by casual contact, such as using a public toilet.

Syphilis occurs in three stages: a primary stage, a secondary stage, and a third, or late, stage. Each stage has unique symptoms. The primary stage occurs ten days to three months after infection. A small sore develops where the spirochete first entered the body. The sore is usually inside the vagina or near the tip of the penis, but sores can also develop in the mouth, around the anus, or in other areas of the body. The sores are open and ooze fluid, but they are usually not painful.

Then the sores usually go away for a while. The person might think he or she is cured. The truth is, syphilis is just waiting for a chance to reappear in a new form. Primary syphilis turns into secondary syphilis.

In its secondary stage, syphilis causes the infected person to break out in a rash. The rash usually appears on the hands, feet, or groin area, but it can develop almost anywhere on the body. The person also develops symptoms resembling the flu. The glands in the neck may swell. The person may feel feverish and achy. These symptoms typically develop weeks or months after the first sore disappears. A person with syphilis can spread the disease easily in both the primary and secondary stages.

At the end of the secondary stage, the disease goes into hiding again and the infected person cannot spread the disease. This time, it can hide for as long as forty years. But when symptoms reappear, they are usually life-threatening. The symptoms of third-stage syphilis vary from person to person.

Syphilis can attack the heart, causing heart failure. It can attack the nervous system, leading to paralysis. If it infects the brain, the person can go insane.[5]

Most people with syphilis are found and cured before the disease reaches this final stage, especially in countries such as the United States where government health care workers monitor the disease very closely. Doctors and nurses who care for pregnant women also check for any signs of syphilis, because the disease can lead to birth defects or kill the baby before it is born.[6]

New Cases of Curable STDs Worldwide[7]

(gonorrhea, chlamydia, syphilis, and trichomoniasis)

South and Southeast Asia	150 million
Sub-Saharan Africa	65 million
Latin America and Caribbean	36 million
East Asia and Pacific	23 million
Eastern Europe and Central Asia	18 million
Western Europe	16 million
North America	14 million
North Africa and Middle East	10 million
Australia and surrounding region	1 million
Total	333 million

Syphilis is diagnosed by a blood test. One syphilis infection does not prevent a person from being infected again. The body does not build up an immunity against the syphilis bacterium.

Gonorrhea: Nothing to "Clap" About

Gonorrhea probably has more nicknames than any other sexually transmitted disease. It has been called the clap, the drip, and the Jack, among other things. It might also be called two-faced. It acts very differently, depending on whether it infects a man or a woman.

Gonorrhea is caused by a bacterium that looks very different from the bacterium that causes syphilis. The germ is shaped like a sphere. Just as with the syphilis bacteria, the gonorrhea bacteria cannot survive very long outside the human body. Gonorrhea, therefore, is almost always passed from person to person during sexual contact, namely vaginal, anal, or oral sex with an infected partner.

If a man is infected with gonorrhea, symptoms appear within two weeks. He will find it very painful to urinate. It will feel as though his penis is burning. There is often a pus-filled discharge along with the urine. Since 95 percent of men with gonorrhea get these very obvious symptoms, most infected men know they need to get treated.

Women, if they have symptoms, will notice a greenish discharge from the vagina and might have pain or burning when they urinate. However, most women infected with gonorrhea do not experience any noticeable symptoms. If a woman's infected sex partner does not tell her about his gonorrhea infection, she will probably not be diagnosed and treated.

Untreated gonorrhea can cause serious problems. In women, the bacteria can spread beyond the vagina up through the reproductive system, infecting other tissues and organs. These infections cause tremendous pain and a condition known as pelvic inflammatory disease (PID). PID is an infection of a woman's reproductive system and affects the uterus and fallopian tubes. A woman with PID can also experience high fever, fatigue, and increased vaginal discharge. PID can be caused by other bacteria as well, but undiagnosed gonorrhea is one of the most common causes.

Men who are not treated can develop infections in the epididymis, a region in the testicles where sperm are stored. These infections can be very painful and require emergency surgery if they spread through the testicles. In rare cases, untreated bacterial infections can lead to male infertility.

Gonorrhea is diagnosed by a type of laboratory test called a cell culture. A doctor will wipe a swab across the penis or vagina, then rub the swab on a small culture dish where bacteria can grow. If the gonorrhea bacteria are present, they will multiply and can be identified under a microscope.

The gonorrhea bacteria can infect a newborn's eyes shortly after birth, leaving the baby blinded for life. If doctors and nurses waited for a lab test to determine if a newborn was infected with gonorrhea, it could be too late. Health care workers do not take any chances. All states require them to use

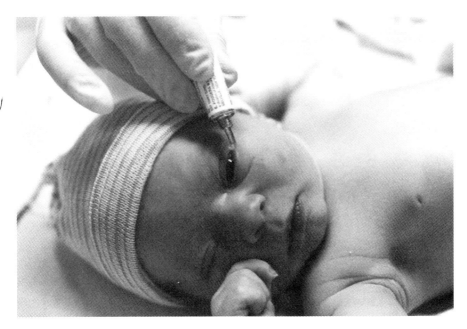

Erythromycin is given to newborns to prevent blindness from chlamydia and gonorrhea. Since the infection can spread so quickly, all infants born in the United States are treated.

antibiotic eyedrops every time a baby is born. It does not matter whether or not they have the disease.[8]

Anyone infected with gonorrhea can get the disease over and over again. The body does not build up an immunity against it.

Chlamydia: America's Leading STD

In 1995, chlamydia became the most common sexually transmitted disease in the United States with almost half a million cases reported to the Centers for Disease Control and Prevention (CDC) in Atlanta. However, the CDC estimates

27

that there are actually more than 4 million new cases of chlamydia in the United States each year.[9]

Chlamydia is caused by a bacterium and is transmitted through sexual contact. The chlamydia bacterium enters the body, latches on to a cell, then moves inside the cell to live and reproduce. (Most other bacteria grow and reproduce on the outside of cells.) Even though chlamydia is living inside cells, it can still be passed to another person by sexual contact. Pregnant women with chlamydia infections can also pass the disease to their babies.

Symptoms usually appear one to four weeks after a person is infected. As with gonorrhea, men are much more likely to have noticeable symptoms. Male symptoms include painful urination, a watery, white discharge from the penis, and pain in the testicles. About one third of men infected with chlamydia will have no symptoms at all.

Only a small number of women show early symptoms of a chlamydia infection. The most common symptom is a heavier vaginal discharge and itch. Women might also experience fever, pain in the lower belly, and burning when they urinate. Chlamydia can occasionally cause spotty bleeding between menstrual periods.

If the infection is not treated promptly, some bacteria might move out to infect other parts of the body. When chlamydia infects the lymph glands, the glands will become swollen and painful. Both men and women can develop a form of arthritis from a long-running infection with chlamydia.

28

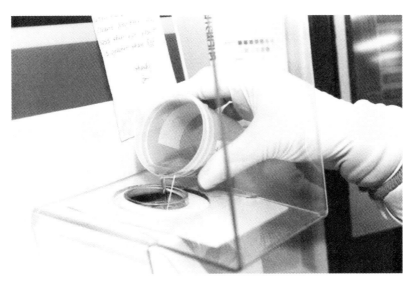

A new test for chlamydia requires only a urine sample, not a blood sample. The test hunts down tiny pieces of chlamydia DNA.

Women are also at high risk of pelvic inflammatory disease (PID) and infertility.[10]

Dr. A. Eugene Washington, who helped to write a major report on sexually transmitted diseases released in 1996, says about 800,000 cases of PID in the United States each year are caused by either chlamydia or gonorrhea. As many as 25 percent of those women will wind up with completely blocked fallopian tubes, the tubes that carry a woman's egg from her ovary to her uterus. That adds up to more than 150,000 cases of infertility each year.[11]

Dr. Washington says teenage girls are at the highest risk of all. "The highest rates are in women below age twenty-five, and the absolute highest rates are in adolescents." In contrast,

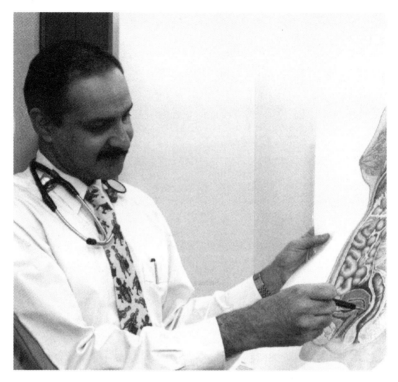

STDs are a leading cause of infertility and ectopic pregnancy in women. The danger comes when the infection spreads farther up the reproductive tract.

the disease tends to be milder and is less likely to spread when the person has been infected more than once.[12]

Newborns are also at risk if their mothers are infected with chlamydia. The disease can cause serious eye infections, blindness, and pneumonia in an infant. Chlamydia also appears to increase the risk that the baby will be born prematurely.[13]

Chlamydia is typically diagnosed by examining cells from an infected person under a microscope. There is no complete immunity to chlamydia. A person can be infected repeatedly.

Chancroid

Chancroid is a sexually transmitted disease that used to be much more widespread but now is quite rare in the United States. It can be confused with syphilis or a viral STD known as herpes, because all three diseases result in sores on the genital organs.

Chancroid is caused by a bacterium. It is passed from one person to another by sexual contact or by contact with an open chancroid sore. A person infected with chancroid can even spread the disease to different parts of his or her own body.

The chancroid sores start out looking like small bumps or boils on the skin. They normally appear on the genital region, inside the mouth, or on the lips. The first symptoms usually show up within one week. Later, the sores split open, which can be painful. If the sores are inside the vagina or around the cervix (the necklike opening to the uterus), a woman might not realize she is infected unless she has a gynecological examination. Some women never even develop sores. They may have other symptoms instead, such as painful urination or an unusual vaginal discharge.[14]

If the disease is not diagnosed and treated, chancroid can spread to the glands in the groin area. This causes tenderness and pain in the infected area. A chancroid infection in the urethra, the tube that carries urine out of the body, can cause serious problems such as disrupting the normal flow of urine.[15]

4

Viral STDs

Wendy Marx was just twenty-two years old when a friend noticed the odd yellow color in her eyes. Marx was not sure what the color meant, but her doctor did. Marx had hepatitis, a viral infection of the liver. Tests quickly showed that she had one of the deadliest forms of hepatitis, hepatitis B. She has no idea how she got the virus. She does know it came within one day of killing her. A liver transplant saved her life.[1]

How Viruses Attack

All viruses share some common features, whether they are sexually transmitted or not. Unlike bacteria, viruses cannot grow or multiply on their own. Viruses are not made of cells and do not contain some of the substances they need to live on their own. They must get their genetic material (DNA or

RNA) inside a body's cell. Once inside, the virus takes control of the cell. The virus "hijacks" the normal body cell, forcing it to make new viral proteins and new copies of the virus's genes. The proteins and genetic material then come together to form offspring of the virus, which leave the cell to infect other cells. Viruses must attach to the outer surface of a cell before they can get inside it. This means they have very specific targets. For example, human immunodeficiency virus, or HIV (the AIDS virus), mainly attacks white blood cells, while hepatitis viruses infect the liver.

The ABCs of Hepatitis

Hepatitis can be caused by many different viruses. Three of them are hepatitis A, hepatitis B, and hepatitis C. Hepatitis B is a hardy virus and is considered an STD because more than half the cases are caused by sexual contact. However, the hepatitis B virus can also be spread by contaminated blood, saliva, or other body fluids. For example, it can be passed from a mother to her baby through breast milk. The instruments used for tattoos, body piercing, and manicures can spread the virus if they are not properly cleaned. Intravenous drug users can get the virus from contaminated needles. Occasionally the virus survives outside the body long enough to be spread by sharing toothbrushes or razors.

The hepatitis virus has one main target in the body. It attacks and destroys the cells of the liver. People infected with hepatitis B do not immediately realize they are sick. Symptoms show up about three weeks to five months after the virus first enters the body. The first signs of hepatitis can often be confused with the flu. The symptoms include fatigue, stomachaches, headaches, and vomiting. Later, the right side of the belly hurts. That is where the main lobe of the liver is located. As the liver stops working normally, a person's eyes and skin turn yellow, the way Wendy Marx's did.

Marx had an acute case of hepatitis. Her symptoms got worse very quickly as the virus destroyed her liver. Many other people infected by hepatitis B or its viral cousin, hepatitis C, do not have such life-threatening episodes. They may not notice any symptoms. The virus can hide in their liver cells for twenty to thirty years.[2] These hepatitis victims are called chronic hepatitis sufferers, but even then the disease can eventually cause cancer or permanent liver damage, including scarring of the liver, called cirrhosis.

Hepatitis A leaves the body in the feces. It is almost always spread by contact with contaminated food and water rather than by sexual contact. For example, people can get sick by eating raw shellfish from areas polluted by raw sewage. Hepatitis A generally causes milder symptoms, including nausea, jaundice, and fatigue. Unlike people with chronic hepatitis B or C, people with hepatitis A recover within a few weeks and never get the disease again. They become immune to the virus.

Blood tests are used to help determine if a person is infected with a hepatitis virus and which form of the virus they have. The test may look for the virus itself or for the antibodies to the virus that have accumulated in the body.

HIV: The Deadliest STD

Human immunodeficiency virus (HIV) is probably the most widely recognized sexually transmitted disease today. The illness AIDS (acquired immunodeficiency syndrome) represents the final stage of HIV infection. Since it was first identified in 1983, HIV has claimed more than 8 million lives. More than 30 million people around the world are infected with HIV.[3] The number of victims is likely to climb for years to come. That fact was hammered home during a World AIDS Day gathering in New York City. An electronic sign in Times Square flashed the warning: "Every second another person is infected with HIV."[4]

Unlike the hepatitis B virus, HIV does not survive very well outside the body. This means that HIV can be spread only by direct contact with contaminated blood, semen, or vaginal fluid. Most cases are spread by sexual contact; however, that is not the only way HIV spreads. Intravenous drug users can spread HIV by sharing contaminated needles. Pregnant women can pass the virus to their babies during pregnancy or during the birth process. The virus can also be passed through breast milk. Very careful screening and testing has greatly reduced the risk from blood transfusions, so very few cases are spread by donated blood or blood products today.

Once HIV gets inside the body, it attacks some of the most important cells of our immune system. They are the white blood cells known as helper T cells. They help our bodies fight off infections from invaders, such as bacteria or viruses, and

"I Did Nothing Wrong"[5]

Kimberly Bergalis was a young woman who "did nothing wrong" but died of AIDS anyway at the age of twenty-three.

Kimberly took good care of herself. Her mother was a nurse. Surely, Kimberly knew exactly what to do to stay healthy. So when she scheduled a visit to her dentist, she had no way of knowing she would come home with the virus that would kill her.

Kimberly Bergalis was the exception, one of the very few people to be infected with HIV by a health care worker. The person responsible was dentist David Acer of Martin County, Florida.

At first, no one believed it was possible, but Kimberly really did have a healthy lifestyle. She never used injected drugs. She never had sex with her boyfriends. She had none of the risk factors associated with HIV.

Finally, tests proved that the virus in Kimberly closely matched the virus found in Dr. Acer. Kimberly begged Congress in September 1991 to pass laws forcing all health care workers to be tested for HIV and to notify their patients if they are infected.

She weighed just seventy pounds when she told Congress, "I did nothing wrong." Three months later, Kimberly Bergalis was dead.

protect us from cancer. A person already infected with one type of STD can more easily be infected by HIV.

Shortly after people are infected with HIV, they usually feel achy and have a slight fever. Often, their necks hurt because their glands are swollen. They might wake up in the middle of the night shivering and sweating. After that time, the virus can hide in the body for several years before any more symptoms occur.

The final stage of the disease is AIDS, marked by the occurrence of a series of clinical conditions and disorders. As a person's immune system is slowly destroyed by HIV, the person will often develop diseases that are usually rare. These are illnesses that healthy people fight easily. Without enough white blood cells, however, a body weakened by HIV cannot fight back. Many of these diseases are caused by fungi or tiny single-celled organisms known as protozoa. People infected with HIV can even develop a rare form of cancer called Kaposi's sarcoma. It causes purple blotches on the skin. HIV can also invade the brain over time, leading to personality changes and dementia—the inability to think or behave normally.[6] Thus, the symptoms of AIDS vary from one person to the next, depending on what illnesses they contract.

Blood tests are used to find out if someone is infected with HIV. The typical test looks for antibodies, special proteins the body produces to fight off infection. However, the test will not work immediately after a person is infected. It takes about three weeks for the body to produce enough antibodies to show up on the test.

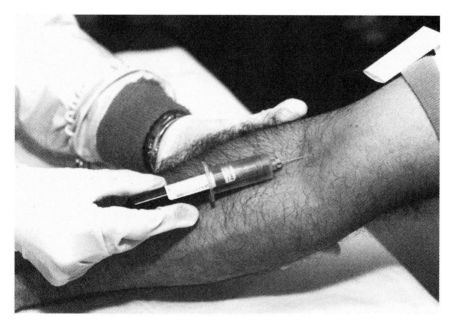

A blood test is used to determine if someone is infected with HIV.

Babies who catch HIV from their mothers often get sick very early in their lives and usually die before their tenth birthday.[7] Basketball star Earvin "Magic" Johnson worried that his baby might develop AIDS. His wife, Cookie, was pregnant when he found out that he had HIV. Fortunately, the virus never spread to his wife, and their baby was born healthy. Johnson still worries about other babies who were not so lucky. In an article about living with HIV, Johnson wrote, "All the people I've met who have had AIDS has affected me. I think the hardest though is all the beautiful children, who are innocent . . . that hurts you the most."[8]

Herpes: The Virus America Forgot

In the early 1980s, very few people understood the great danger of the HIV epidemic. Instead, the news media in the United States were up in arms over another sexually transmitted virus. Headline after headline warned about the dangers of genital herpes.[9] The hype was so great that a character in the 1983 movie *The Big Chill* even joked that he had given up his freewheeling sexual lifestyle because of a fear of herpes. The fear of HIV has replaced the fear of herpes, but herpes remains a major threat.

There are two types of herpes simplex viruses. Cold sores or fever blisters are usually caused by herpes simplex virus type one (HSV-1). Genital herpes is usually caused by the herpes simplex virus type two (HSV-2). Both HSV-1 and HSV-2 can be transmitted during sexual contact. The viruses are normally spread when they are active, causing an outbreak of sores. But if the outbreak is mild, a person can spread the virus without realizing he or she is contagious.

Any contact with a herpes sore can spread the disease. The virus can also be transmitted through saliva, so it is possible to catch herpes by kissing someone or through oral sex.[10] People who are infected with herpes simplex viruses without showing any symptoms can also spread the disease.

The symptoms of the herpesvirus are usually hard to miss. Herpes causes painful blisters or sores in the genital region or other parts of the body that come in contact with the virus. The sores first appear between two days and two weeks after a person is infected. If the sores are inside a woman's vagina, there may also be a discharge. The first outbreak is usually the most painful, but the virus hides in the body and can cause many more outbreaks in the future. Later outbreaks often start with itching or redness, followed by fluid-filled blisters. Each outbreak lasts about three weeks. The virus stays in the body for an entire lifetime.[11]

Newborns are at very great risk if their mothers have an active HSV-2 infection at the time they are born. The babies can have birth defects, grow up mentally retarded, or even die.[12]

To find out if someone has herpes, laboratory tests must be done on scrapings from the blisters or sores. In women, the virus can be found during a routine cancer screening known as a Pap smear. The smear is a sample of cells taken from the woman's cervix. A laboratory worker examines the cells under a microscope.

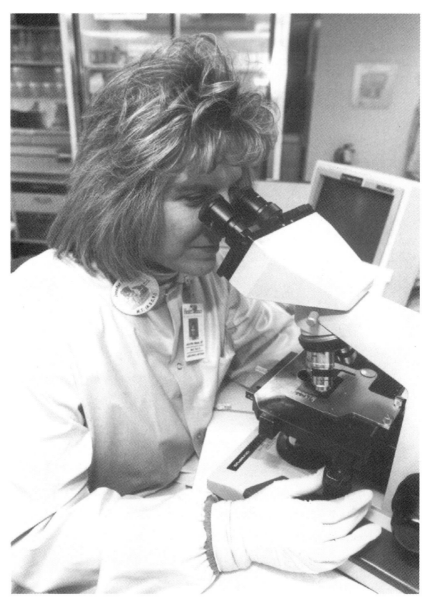

A medical technician examines a slide for signs of cervical cancer.

HPV and Genital Warts

The human papillomavirus (HPV) is a sexually transmitted virus that does not show its worst effects until years after the first infection. In the early stages of infection, HPV can cause genital warts, which are also known as condylomas. Eight to ten years later, the same virus can cause cancer.

There are over seventy strains of HPV, and at least fifteen of them can cause genital warts. Two strains are considered high risk because they are closely linked with the development of cancer in men and women.[13] The viruses are spread by direct sexual contact with an infected individual. Warts do not have to be visible for HPV to spread. HPV usually gets inside the body through tiny scrapes in the genital area. In women, the virus usually gets inside the cells of the cervix, where the tissue is very thin. A pregnant woman infected with HPV can pass the virus to her baby during birth.

The key symptom of an HPV infection is the development of genital warts. The warts can be many different colors, including white, pink, or brown. They can be so small you need a microscope to see them, or they can form large clusters that resemble cauliflower. They may show up within a month or up to several years after the infection. The warts are normally found in the genital region or around the anus, but HPV can also cause warts in the mouth or throat.

Many people with genital warts never notice a thing. In women, the warts might grow inside the vagina or on the cervix, where the victim would not notice them.[14]

Doctors can diagnose an HPV infection by examining the warts, if any are present. A solution of vinegar can be used to make tiny warts more visible. The vinegar is acidic and turns infected tissues white.[15] HPV infections in women can be diagnosed through a Pap smear. One HPV infection does not prevent future infections. A person can be infected many times. HPV might also go into remission, but can reappear later in life.

Researchers now believe that 90 percent of all cases of cervical cancer are caused by the human papillomavirus (HPV), the virus that causes genital warts. Cancer may also develop in the vagina or in the vulva, the folds of skin at the entrance to the vagina. In men, HPV can lead to cancer of the penis. It is also possible for HPV to cause cancer around the anus in both men and women.[16]

5

Other STDs

lthough many sexually transmitted diseases are caused by bacteria or viruses, there are several STDs that are not. The following are examples of nonviral and nonbacterial diseases that can be spread by sexual contact.

Trichomoniasis: A Worldwide Threat

Trichomoniasis is a sexually transmitted disease that makes millions of people sick each year; however, very few people know anything about the disease. There are roughly 3 million cases in the United States each year.[1] Worldwide, it is by far the most common of all curable STDs.[2]

The disease is caused by a tiny parasite called *Trichomonas*, or "trich" for short. *Trichomonas* is a protozoan, a single-celled parasite that uses a tail-like structure called a flagellum to swim around.[3] The parasite can survive for several hours outside of the body as long as it has some water. Therefore, trichomoniasis can be spread both by sexual contact and by casual contact. Casual contact includes contact with towels, bedding, or even toilet seats used by a person with trichomoniasis. Newborn babies can be infected if their mothers have the disease.

Unlike many other types of sexually transmitted diseases, men are much more likely to get trichomoniasis without noticing any symptoms. When symptoms do occur, a man usually notices a burning or painful feeling when he urinates. Women with a *Trichomonas* infection often notice a foul-smelling, oddly colored discharge from the vagina. They may also have a burning or itching feeling around the opening to the vagina.[4] If a pregnant woman has the disease, her baby might be born too early or too small.[5]

Samples of secretions from the vagina are taken to determine if a woman is infected with *Trichomonas*. The samples are studied under a microscope to see if the parasite is present or not.

Pubic Lice

Pubic lice or crab lice are tiny insects that live on the hair in the genital region and can spread to other hairy parts of the body. They are not the same as head lice, although both types of lice cause a great deal of itching. Pubic lice can be spread by sexual contact, but they are commonly spread by casual contact. Casual contact includes contact with a washcloth, toilet seat, or bedding used by a person infected with pubic lice.

The Impact of STDs in the United States

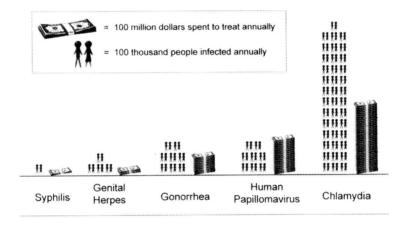

Sexually transmitted diseases cost the United States billions of dollars every year.

Intense itching is usually the only symptom people notice. The female louse lays her eggs on the shaft of the hair, where the eggs are very difficult to remove. The disease is usually diagnosed by finding the eggs.

Scabies

Scabies are also known as itch mites. They are related to spiders. Scabies can be transmitted during sexual contact, but, like pubic lice, the infection can spread without sexual activity. Generally though, prolonged skin-to-skin contact with an infected person is necessary to get the disease.

The scabies mite burrows under the skin, causing a rash. The rash can spread to the arms, stomach, or chest. These symptoms appear two to six weeks after a person is first infected. If a person gets the disease again, symptoms appear much faster—the person will notice the itching and rash within a few days. A doctor can spot signs of a scabies infection during a physical examination.

Candidiasis (Yeast Infections)

Candida is a yeast (a type of fungus) that normally lives in the vagina and can be found in the mouth and intestines as well. Occasionally, though, the yeast can grow out of control, leading to an infection called candidiasis. If the infection occurs in the mouth, it is called thrush. A person taking antibiotics to treat a bacterial infection or a person with a weakened immune system is more likely to get a *Candida* infection, because his or her body cannot keep the yeast from growing out of control. For example, candidiasis is one of the most common infections among HIV patients.

Women with a vaginal yeast infection experience vaginal itching and discomfort. There might also be a heavy, white-colored discharge from the vagina. These symptoms are similar to the symptoms of many other sexually transmitted diseases, so it is important for the infection to be diagnosed by a doctor before treatment begins. Genital yeast infections in men usually affect the scrotum, which is the tissue surrounding the testicles.

A yeast infection of the genitals is diagnosed by examining secretions from the vagina or penis under a microscope. A physical examination of the vagina might also show distinctive white patches, which are typical of a yeast infection.

Trichomoniasis, pubic lice, scabies, and candidiasis are all conditions that can reoccur. They can be passed back and forth between sexual partners. Getting trichomoniasis, pubic lice, scabies, or candidiasis once does not protect a person from being reinfected.

6

Treating STDs

"G o away! Go away!" the woman hollered over and over again at the nurse from the local health department. The woman had been a patient once, needing treatment for syphilis. Now she was afraid the health department was after her.

"She was standing on a street corner as I was trying to parallel park my car," recalls nurse Laura Alexoff. "I saw her and waved. She thought I was tracking her down and started hollering. I told her I wasn't coming to see her. I was going to check on somebody else."[1]

Laura Alexoff worked in some of Cincinnati's poorest neighborhoods as a public health nurse. Her job—giving shots and medication when someone was diagnosed with a sexually transmitted disease—was not easy. "Many of them didn't want to see you. They'd be in denial or thought they could handle it on their own."[2]

Treating the Problem Together

Health care workers all over the country face similar problems. It is very difficult to get people with sexually transmitted diseases to come in for treatment. It is even more difficult to get their sex partners treated. To be effective, both partners must be treated together.

Certified nurse/midwife Jane Vandervort says many patients are too stunned, scared, or angry to think about treatment right away. "The woman will wonder, 'Did he give it to me? Did I give it to him?' We try to emphasize that it really doesn't matter. The important thing is to get treatment."[3]

There are medications available to treat many sexually transmitted infections, but many STD victims believe if they feel healthy, they do not need medicine. They believe that it does not matter what the test results say and it does not matter what their sex partner tells them. "Many won't even come into the clinic for the medicine if they're not having symptoms," said Vandervort. "They don't understand how important it is."[4]

What is really frustrating for health care workers is when a pregnant woman will not tell her husband or boyfriend that she has a sexually transmitted disease. The woman may be cured in a matter of weeks, but since her sex partner was not treated, she gets the infection all over again. "It's hard for them to understand the partner must be treated too. So they often wind up reinfecting each other," said Vandervort.[5] For example, one eighteen-year-old woman wound up with four different infections over the course of her pregnancy, including trichomoniasis, HPV, chlamydia, and gonorrhea.[6]

The Battle Against Bacteria

The discovery of penicillin in 1943 gave doctors their first effective weapon against sexually transmitted diseases caused by bacteria, such as syphilis and gonorrhea. To treat syphilis, penicillin is usually given in a series of shots or injections to make sure the syphilis spirochetes are all killed. If a baby catches syphilis from its mother during childbirth, the baby must be treated quickly to avoid serious problems.

Penicillin does not always work against gonorrhea. The bacterium that causes gonorrhea has evolved. Today, there are many strains of gonorrhea that cannot be killed by penicillin or tetracycline, another common antibiotic. America's top STD experts are worried.

"This is a serious situation," said Joan Knapp, the chief of molecular epidemiology for sexually transmitted diseases at the Centers for Disease Control and Prevention (CDC). "There aren't many drugs left that still work against this bug."[7] The CDC has found highly resistant gonorrhea in Honolulu, Denver, and Seattle. Health care workers in Canada have found similar resistant strains in Quebec. Apparently, some of those new forms of gonorrhea came from Southeast Asia, where there is also a serious problem with resistant gonorrhea.[8]

Dr. Bradley Stoner of the Washington University School of Medicine in St. Louis says resistant strains of bacteria often show up when health workers in one area rely too much on just one type of antibiotic. Unfortunately, once resistance develops in one area, those bacteria can spread to other communities as well. Dr. Stoner also says some antibiotics are too dangerous to use on certain patients. For example, the antibiotics known as quinolones should not be used by pregnant women or people under the age of eighteen.[9]

Gonorrhea is usually treated with antibiotics that work in just one dose. Chancroid and chlamydia infections are usually

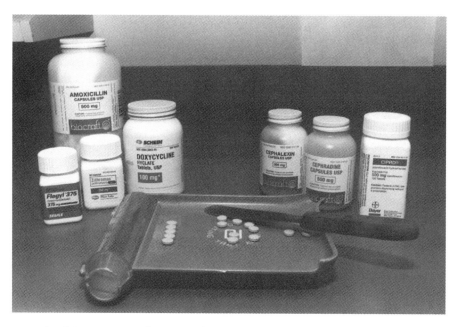

Antibiotics are used to treat bacterial STDs. Gonorrhea has become resistant to many of them.

treated with different antibiotics. These antibiotics need to be taken in several doses over several days to clear up the infection. People infected with bacterial STDs need to be treated at a doctor's office or health care facility so that the proper medicine and course of treatment can be determined. The sex partners of individuals diagnosed with a bacterial STD should be treated with antibiotics, even if they do not have any symptoms.

It is very important to take all of the prescribed medication, even when the symptoms disappear. If a person does not finish the treatment, the disease can come back. If one antibiotic does not work, doctors will change the prescription to a different one. No matter what, a person should never take someone else's antibiotics. Only a doctor or STD expert should decide what is the proper treatment.

Fighting Viruses

Viruses behave differently in the body, so viral STDs must be treated differently from bacterial STDs. Most treatments for viral STDs only help people feel more comfortable. The treatments do not actually cure the disease because they cannot kill the individual viruses.

Prescription for Hepatitis: Rest, Relax, and Hope

There is no effective drug to treat hepatitis A, B, or C. Most people simply fight off the virus on their own. It is important for someone infected with hepatitis to get plenty of rest, because the liver damage done by hepatitis makes a person feel tired all the time.

If rest and relaxation do not work, a drug called interferon can be used to help a person fight off a hepatitis infection. Interferon is an immune-boosting protein normally produced by the human body to fight viruses. The drug interferon is a

Who Is at Risk?[10]

Highest rates of gonorrhea
Georgia, Louisiana, Maryland, North Carolina, South Carolina, and Tennessee

Highest rates of chlamydia
Maryland, New Mexico, South Carolina, Tennessee, and Texas

Highest rates of AIDS
California, Florida, Maryland, New Jersey, and New York

Syphilis rates
Nearly sixty times higher in blacks than in whites

Age groups at highest risk in U.S.
AIDS	25–39
Gonorrhea	15–24
Syphilis	25–39

copy of that natural protein. It works like a chemical alarm, warning cells that a virus is present in the body. The warning makes it harder for the hepatitis virus to infect other cells.

Standard Care for HIV Patients

The United States Public Health Service now recommends a three-pronged approach to treating a person infected with HIV. First, the patient receives drugs that directly attack HIV, making it more difficult for the virus to make new copies of itself. Second, the patient receives medication to help prevent new opportunistic infections from occurring. Finally, the patient receives drugs to treat any opportunistic infections that are already present. It is common for a patient with HIV to be taking five to seven different drugs at once.

There are many new drugs to fight HIV, and people infected with HIV fought hard to get them. AIDS patients have been one of the loudest and most active patient groups in this country, lobbying Congress and other agencies for quick access to the latest anti-HIV drugs and increased funding for HIV research. Their efforts paid off with many new types of drugs and a new strategy for treating those infected with HIV.

Cocktail Therapy and HIV

There have been drugs to treat HIV available since the late 1980s, but one-on-one, HIV always came out ahead. The virus would mutate, or change, into a resistant form that could not be harmed by the drug.[11] In 1996 *Time* magazine named Dr. David Ho its Man of the Year for pioneering cocktail therapy at the Aaron Diamond AIDS Research Center in New York City. Dr. Ho's cocktail approach combined several different anti-HIV drugs that attack HIV in different ways. It is the most effective method found so far to treat an HIV infection, although drug resistance remains a concern.

"Ten billion viruses are produced every day in a person, so the virus can become resistant very quickly," explains Dr. Pablo Tebas, who tests new AIDS drugs at the Washington University School of Medicine in St. Louis. Dr. Tebas says cocktail therapy can greatly reduce the amount of HIV in a person's body, but it does not completely cure it. Cocktail therapy will not work for all those infected with HIV. Some people have severe side effects such as nausea and diarrhea. The new protease inhibitors can cause painful kidney stones as well.[12] Still, cocktail therapy has been so successful in the United States that the death rate from AIDS dropped 44 percent in 1997.[13]

The first type of drug used in cocktail therapy is called a reverse transcriptase inhibitor, or RT inhibitor. Reverse transcriptase is the enzyme that turns the genetic material of the virus (RNA) into another form of genetic material (DNA). The viral DNA becomes part of the infected cell, taking control and forcing the cell to make hundreds of new viruses.

RT inhibitors, such as AZT (the first anti-AIDS drug), fool the enzyme. They look like normal DNA building blocks, but when they are hooked on to a chain of DNA, DNA production stops.

Three Targets of Anti-HIV Drugs

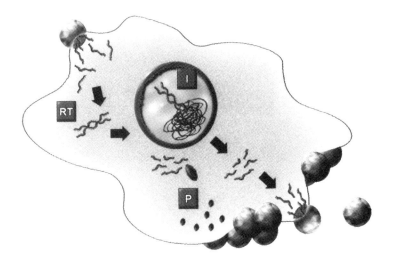

Researchers are trying to attack HIV at different phases in its life cycle. Currently available drugs inhibit the enzymes reverse transcriptase (RT) and protease (P). A third group of drugs that inhibit the integrase (I) enzyme is under development. All three enzymes must work in order for HIV to reproduce.

The newest drugs being used in combination with RT inhibitors are drugs that inhibit the enzyme protease.

The new drug is a very effective partner with the older RT inhibitors. "It's a very potent and very important drug and has changed the way we treat patients," said Dr. Tebas.[14] The combination therapy has been so effective, the federal government changed its recommendations for AIDS treatment in 1997. A three-drug cocktail, including one protease inhibitor and two RT inhibitors, is now the preferred method of treating people infected with HIV.[15]

A Simpler Way to Treat Herpes

Medicines such as acyclovir can reduce the symptoms of herpes, make a person's sores go away faster, and possibly reduce the number of flare-ups. But once a person is infected with the herpesvirus, he or she is infected for life.

The medicine is applied on the sores as an ointment or taken in a pill form. The ointments are inconvenient, because they are messy and often soak into a person's underwear. The pills are inconvenient to take because an infected person needs to take the medication up to five times a day. "You walk down the street, and you're rattling," complained one herpes victim.[16]

New versions of herpes drugs are now being tested. Because more of the drug is absorbed by the body, the new drugs can be used in lower doses and less often. Researchers hope a herpes patient will eventually need only one pill a day. If that happens, more people might get treated for herpes. Right now, most people suffer through herpes flare-ups without taking any medication at all.

A New Drug to Fight Genital Warts

The United States Food and Drug Administration (FDA) decides if a drug is safe and effective enough to be used in this country. In 1997, the FDA approved the first new treatment for genital warts in five years. It is an ointment that is spread on the infected areas. The ointment does not kill the human papillomavirus (HPV) that causes the warts, but it can eliminate the warts.[17]

The other way to treat genital warts is to remove them. Doctors can use lasers, chemicals, or surgery to destroy the warts. It is also possible to freeze the warts to destroy them. These treatments can all be very painful, and the warts can grow back if any virus remains in the body.

Tricking *Trichomonas*

A person infected with *Trichomonas* requires a special medication because *Trichomonas* is a protozoan, not a bacterium or a virus. The most commonly used drug against *Trichomonas* is called Flagyl. It is a very powerful medicine that can cause nausea and headaches. The drug is taken in pill form, and people who are being treated are warned not to drink alcohol because it interferes with the medicine.

Treating Other Genital Infections

Even though pubic lice live in the hair around the penis or vagina, shaving is not enough to get rid of the lice. A person must use a lotion or shampoo that contains an insecticide such as lindane or permethrin. These products can be toxic and must be used exactly as directed. Permethrin and lindane lotions and shampoos are also used to treat scabies.

For both lice and scabies, any clothes, towels, or bedding that might be contaminated must be washed in very hot water

61

and dried at the highest possible temperature to prevent new infections.

After diagnosis by a doctor, yeast infections can be treated with over-the-counter ointments. A doctor can prescribe stronger medications if necessary. Some of these medicines are contained in capsules called suppositories, which are inserted inside the vagina to release the medicine slowly over time.

Treatments That Do Not Work

Nurse Kathy Sabin worries most about patients like André in the beginning of this book who try to treat themselves, using home remedies or the wrong type of drugs.[18] Delaying proper medical treatment can lead to much more serious infections and complications.

Sabin says many girls actually put themselves at greater risk by using vaginal rinses called douches. The girls think the douches will protect them from STDs and pregnancy, but they do not work that way. "Douches wash away normal bacteria, so there's more of an opportunity for the STD organisms to grow. They thought it was cleansing. It can actually cause infections," warns Sabin.[19] Simply put, douches cannot cure or prevent sexually transmitted infections. Home remedies do not work.

7

STDs in Society

When most people think about infectious diseases, they think about their last cold or the flu that has been going around at school or work. The government cannot keep track of all those diseases, but it does keep track of what it considers the most dangerous infectious diseases. Reports come in from health departments all over the country, and government health workers at the Centers for Disease Control and Prevention count all the cases of each disease.

When you look at the most frequently reported infectious diseases in the United States, 87 percent are sexually transmitted diseases. There are 12 million new cases each year. STDs are clearly a big problem in society, but one of the biggest problems is that no one likes to talk about them. The Institute of Medicine is a branch of the National Academy of Sciences in Washington, D.C., which helps advise the United States government on issues of medical care, research, and education. Researchers who studied the problem of STDs for the Institute of Medicine call sexually transmitted diseases America's "hidden epidemic," and they say we need to do a lot more to educate people and prevent these dangerous diseases.[1]

Fear of AIDS

The fear of AIDS has made a big difference in the classroom. Panicked parents and school leaders forced young hemophiliacs like Ryan White in Indiana and Ricky, Randy, and Robert Ray of Florida to leave school.[2] Each young boy caught HIV from contaminated blood. Experts were sure the boys could go to school without harming any of their classmates, but expert opinions were ignored. No one was taking any chances with such a deadly disease.

Today, Ryan White is remembered as a hero. He fought back against the stigma and against the prejudice toward people with HIV. He fought in court until a judge said he could go back to school. In 1990, at just eighteen years old, Ryan White died. But his fight continues. There is now a federal law called the Ryan White Act that provides money to fight the disease that killed the young man.[3]

On the other hand, concern over HIV helps those trying to spread the word about other sexually transmitted diseases. "STDs are not really high on the list [of topics] that school administrators want their teachers to talk about," said Deborah Schoeberlein, executive director of Redefining Actions and Decisions, a nonprofit group in Colorado that develops educational material about sexually transmitted diseases. "HIV has opened the door to allow educators to include the discussion of other diseases. AIDS is a pretty potent motivator, and that's helpful for education."[4]

The Stigma of Other STDs

Other sexually transmitted diseases carry their own stigmas. With viral diseases such as herpes, the stigma lasts a lifetime because the virus never goes away. "It's a brand, a disgrace, a reproach," said Gay Baynes, a therapist who works with herpes patients. Baynes says patients often feel angry or contaminated when they find out they are infected. They often avoid sex because they are so embarrassed by their disease.[5]

Tuskegee Study

The Tuskegee Study, which ran from 1932 until 1972 under the control of the United States Public Health Service, showed how some victims of sexually transmitted diseases were treated differently from others. Six hundred black men in rural Alabama took part in the study. The doctors knew that 399 of them had syphilis. They all reported dutifully for medical testing for years so that doctors and nurses could monitor the progress of their disease. However, the men were never told that they had syphilis.

These patients did not really understand their role in the study. For example, many of the men were given painful spinal taps. Large needles were inserted into their backbones to draw out fluid to see if the syphilis bacteria had spread into their nervous systems. The doctors deliberately tricked the men, telling them the needles were part of their treatment.[6] The government-sponsored doctors and nurses did virtually nothing to cure or treat the disease. As a result, at least forty of the men's wives and nineteen children were infected over the years.[7]

Many southern black soldiers may have been infected with syphilis during World War I. Many of the doctors at the time of the Tuskegee Study believed that black lifestyle was to blame for their disease. These doctors believed blacks were too ignorant, too immoral, and too poor to deserve proper care.[8] This belief may have been one reason the black men in the

Many of the participants in the Tuskegee Study came to the John A. Andrews Hospital in Tuskegee, Alabama, for tests and medical exams.

study were treated so poorly. Today, it would be impossible to do such a study in the United States. The controversy over the Tuskegee Study helped to bring about strict new rules on human research.

In 1997, United States President Bill Clinton finally apologized to the few victims still alive. Clinton said the doctors "did something that was wrong—deeply, profoundly, morally wrong."[9] Four survivors and their families were on hand to listen to President Clinton. The oldest was one-hundred-year-old Fred Simmons. He said he accepted the President's apology.

Clusters of Cases

Different groups of people can become associated with a particular sexually transmitted disease because of the way the disease may cluster in a particular area or community. For example, syphilis is a bigger problem in the inner city and in the southeastern United States. Hepatitis B is most common in the western states. When most cases of a particular STD come from one particular area, scientists call this the "core group phenomenon." Syphilis and gonorrhea are typical of the core group phenomenon.[10]

Homosexual men suffer from the stigma of HIV because in the United States the disease was first discovered in homosexual men. Today, HIV is found in all age groups and all cultures. In 1997, nearly half of all AIDS deaths worldwide were in women.[11] The number of minorities infected is increasing. Despite the statistics, many people still consider HIV to be a "gay" disease. The stigma remains.

Who Is Sexually Active?[12]

Black high school students

Males	81 percent
Females	67 percent

Hispanic high school students

Males	62 percent
Females	53 percent

White high school students

Males	49 percent
Females	49 percent

The Impact on Women

Women suffer both physically and socially from sexually transmitted diseases. The British Contagious Disease Acts of the 1860s were just one example of discrimination against women with STDs. The laws punished only women, not men. People who thought the laws were unfair fought to have them changed, and the acts were repealed in 1886. However, the stigma remained. Women were still more likely than men to be scorned or ridiculed if they caught an STD.[13]

Physically, women are more likely than men to be infected because of differences in the female reproductive tract. The warm, moist environment of the vagina and cervix makes it easy for bacteria to grow and for other sexually transmitted organisms to survive. The walls of the vagina and thin surface of the cervix are also likely to be scraped slightly during sexual intercourse or intimate sexual contact. That makes it easy for microbes to invade a woman's body and cause a disease.

Women also suffer more long-term effects from STDs because they often do not discover they are infected until serious complications such as pelvic inflammatory disease (PID) occur. "Women don't know [that they may have an STD] because their partners don't tell them," said Dr. A. Eugene Washington, a specialist in women's reproductive health and a professor at the University of California, San Francisco. "One Bay Area woman had [rampant] PID, but she didn't appear to be in a high-risk group, so no one suspected an STD. Now she's infertile. Infertility is one of the serious, sad outcomes."[14]

Infertility occurs because bacterial infections can leave scars in the narrow fallopian tubes. The scars can also leave a woman at high risk of an ectopic pregnancy. In an ectopic pregnancy, the baby grows in the wrong place, somewhere outside the uterus. The baby cannot survive outside the uterus, and the mother may also die if the condition is not diagnosed quickly enough.

The Poor and the Young

Scientists have deduced that minorities have higher rates of sexually transmitted diseases than whites. There is no biological reason for this, but minorities do have a disadvantage. Many blacks and Hispanics do not have access to quality health care.[15] People living in poverty anywhere in the world are at great risk of developing STDs and complications from untreated sexually transmitted diseases.[16]

The World Health Organization blamed an increase in prostitution and unemployment for an "alarming" increase in HIV and other STD infections in the former Soviet Union. For example, the rate of new syphilis cases in Russia during 1996 was one hundred times higher than the average in Western Europe, where economic conditions were better.[17]

People who use drugs and alcohol are also at higher risk for getting an STD. Drugs and alcohol are common in poor neighborhoods, but teenagers are at risk, too. Teens who drink and use drugs are more likely to be sexually active and are less likely to use condoms. Their behavior puts them at greater risk.[18] Teenagers are at a higher biological risk, too. They have higher levels of sex hormones in their blood than mature adults. These hormones cause changes in the body that make it easier for STD microbes to invade.[19]

A lack of money is making it difficult to help many victims of sexually transmitted diseases. The promising new drugs to fight HIV will never be available for most AIDS patients worldwide. Drug companies can make enough of the drug, but the drugs are so expensive that very few people can afford them. Cocktail therapy can cost $20,000 a year, far too much money for 90 percent of the people living in less developed parts of the world.[20]

But even in the United States, there is a limit to the amount of free or low-cost medical treatment available to

Experts say high school is too late to begin educating students about sex and sexually transmitted diseases.

people without health insurance. For example, in some rural counties, a man infected with a sexually transmitted disease has to drive to the next county to get treated.

When Individuals Fight Back

The biggest change in the fight against sexually transmitted diseases is the fight going on in many courtrooms around the country. Spreading sexually transmitted diseases is not just unhealthy. Some people think it is a crime. An American man who had sex with dozens of women in Finland without telling them he was infected with HIV was charged with attempted murder.[21]

In California, women have sued men for lying about their STD status. One woman trusted her new sex partner. He confidently told her he did not have HIV, knowing he was infected with a different STD, genital herpes. Now she has herpes, too. She came down with an extremely painful case of sores and a fever. She could not walk, sit, or use the bathroom without feeling terrible pain. She went to court, using the name Jane Doe to protect her privacy. The man gave up before the case went to trial, agreeing to pay damages to the woman.[22]

Another court awarded over three hundred thousand dollars to a school administrator whose new husband had herpes. She specifically asked if he had an STD and was assured he did not. Less than one year later, she found the medicine he used to keep his herpes under control. He not only lost his money, he also lost his new wife.[23]

8

Preventing STDs

At first glance, preventing sexually transmitted diseases looks easy. A person can avoid sex or use a condom. In the real world, it is just not that simple.

"I guess I thought love would protect me," says eighteen-year-old Carrie. Carrie thought she knew how to play it safe. She never gave in to pressure to have sex in high school. She was going to wait. When she turned eighteen, she fell in love. Her boyfriend was nice, not the type of boy, she thought, who could possibly have a sexually transmitted disease. Carrie was wrong. Shortly after beginning a sexual relationship, Carrie got chlamydia.[1]

William Butler, chancellor of the Baylor College of Medicine and chairman of the Institute of Medicine Committee on Prevention and Control of Sexually Transmitted Diseases, says we need to start fighting back against STDs. "We need . . . to promote healthy sexual behaviors, protect adolescents, provide high-quality clinical services, and energize strong leadership in the fight against STDs," he said on the day the committee released its report, called "The Hidden Epidemic," in November 1996.[2] Butler was especially concerned about STD victims like Carrie, because women and children are at the greatest risk.

"Please Use a Condom"

South Africa has so many people infected with HIV and other sexually transmitted diseases that Nobel Peace Prize winner Archbishop Desmond Tutu went on national television to urge people to "please use a condom." Tutu made it clear that the church expects people to abstain from sex until marriage, but he also made it clear that he is very worried about the huge numbers of people dying from AIDS.[3]

Dr. Bradley Stoner of the Washington University School of Medicine in St. Louis is worried, too. He sees more and more teenagers being treated for sexually transmitted diseases. That is frustrating, because Dr. Stoner knows the diseases can be prevented so easily. "Condoms prevent transmission of STDs. It is as simple as that. Most people do not like condoms . . . but when used properly they do work."[4]

Studies show that Dr. Stoner is right. Laboratory tests indicate latex condoms can prevent the spread of chlamydia, gonorrhea, genital herpes, hepatitis B, and HIV.[5] Although condoms can break, breakage is very rare. Less than 2 percent of condoms break during use, and this usually only happens when the instructions are not followed.[6]

His or Her Condoms

Condoms have been available for males since the sixteenth century, when men would wrap thin cloth around their penises to protect themselves from syphilis. Today, condoms are made from lambskin, latex, or polyurethane. Lambskin condoms do not protect as well as the other two types. Latex condoms are the least expensive of the three types. They often cost less than fifty cents each. However, some people are allergic to latex. They can use a polyurethane condom instead.[7]

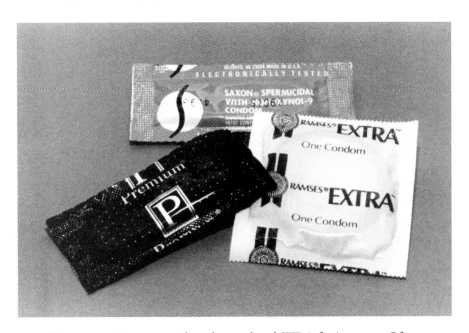

Programs to give away condoms have reduced STD infection rates. Often, the programs stir up controversy in local communities.

Women who cannot get their sex partner to use a condom now have another option. Since 1993, a female condom has been available in the United States. It is larger than a male condom and fits inside the vagina, secured by two flexible rings. The female condom protects a woman from both pregnancy and sexually transmitted diseases.

The female condom is not widely used yet in the United States, but many other countries are eager to make it available for STD prevention. The Female Health Company, which created the female condom, is working with the Joint United Nations Program on HIV/AIDS (UNAIDS) to supply female condoms at a bargain price for public health prevention programs. The UNAIDS program will serve nearly two hundred countries around the world.[8]

Women in Zimbabwe did not wait for the United Nations to get involved. They went directly to their government, demanding that the government make female condoms readily available. Priscilla Misihairabwi of Zimbabwe's Women and AIDS Support Network says men will not use male condoms, so women must have a way to protect themselves. "Surveys done here [in Zimbabwe] show that both men and women prefer the female condom to the male one, so we are petitioning the government to make it freely available and affordable," Misihairabwi said.[9]

Condom Availability in the United States

Making condoms readily available in the United States does not always get strong support from local government leaders.

National polls show that 75 percent of adult Americans believe condoms are useful, but their support usually stops when the school bell rings.[10] Less than 3 percent of all the high schools in the United States provide condoms. This small number reflects the controversy surrounding this issue. Wachusett Regional High School in Worcester, Massachusetts, installed a condom machine but removed it in 1994 following a bitter debate between parents and school officials. The debate never really ended. Two years later, a group of students, teachers, and parents were back before the school board with a petition signed by seven hundred people. They wanted their condom machine back.[11]

Condom Use in U.S. Teens*[12]

Males	60.5 percent
Females	48.6 percent
Total	54.4 percent
Blacks	66.1 percent
Hispanics	52.5 percent
Whites	44.4 percent
Ninth-grade girls	58.5 percent
Twelfth-grade girls	43.1 percent

*teens who reported using a condom or having their sex partner use a condom during their last sexual intercourse

Louisiana public health officials use a different strategy to fight back against sexually transmitted disease. They began a program to make condoms readily available to the general public in areas where STD rates are high. The program relies on more than one thousand businesses, including hundreds of convenience stores and bars. More than 20 million condoms were handed out in two years. More important, gonorrhea rates in Louisiana dropped significantly since the program began.[13]

Beyond the Condom

The condom is not the only method of birth control that protects against sexually transmitted diseases. There is some evidence that contraceptive foams and gels protect women from STDs such as gonorrhea and chlamydia. In the laboratory, the active spermicide in those foams and gels also kills the germs that cause syphilis, herpes, AIDS, and trichomoniasis.[14] However, the Food and Drug Administration does not believe the medicine works as well inside the vagina as it does in the laboratory. The spermicides can be irritating, which can actually make it easier for germs to start an infection. In addition, the gels and foams seem to work only about half the time. "There have been very conflicting research results on the effectiveness of spermicides. No one is formally recommending their use to prevent STDs," says Dorothy Mann, Executive Director of the Family Planning Council of Philadelphia.[15]

The Only Effective STD Vaccine

There is only one vaccine being sold today that is proven to protect people against a sexually transmitted disease. It is a vaccine for hepatitis B. To be fully protected, a person needs to get three shots over a period of six months. That makes it difficult for health care workers planning prevention efforts.

Seattle area health care workers developed a program to protect as many sexually active teenagers as possible. They offered free hepatitis B vaccinations to teenagers who came into health clinics to be treated for other STDs. Nearly

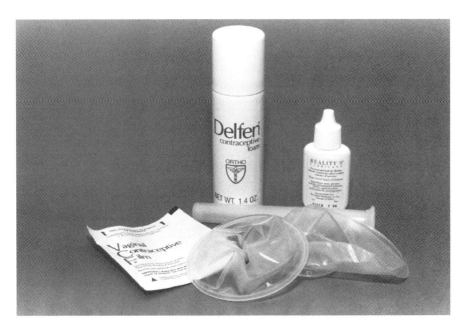

Women can protect themselves with the new female condom. Contraceptive foams and gels have spermicides that can kill STD microbes in the lab, but may not work as well inside the body.

twenty-five hundred teenagers got the first shot, but only 33 percent got all three doses.[16]

Treating children with the hepatitis B vaccine does appear to prevent infections and complications from hepatitis very effectively. Taiwan began vaccinating all children in 1984. Hepatitis B can lead to liver cancer, and the liver cancer rate in children has dropped significantly since the vaccination program began.[17]

Additional Safeguards for Individuals

In addition to using a condom during sexual intercourse and getting vaccinated against hepatitis B, there are a few common-sense precautions to prevent a sexually transmitted disease infection. It is important to find out as much as possible about a potential sex partner's history to see if they might have been exposed to an STD. Also, if someone is bleeding, treat the blood as if it were contaminated. Using rubber gloves and disinfecting contaminated material with bleach can protect a person from blood contaminated with either HIV or the hepatitis viruses. Health care workers and rescue workers already do these things. The practices are called universal precautions.

Partner Notification

To prevent the spread of STDs, it is critical that an infected person notify his or her sexual partner so that the disease does not continue to be passed back and forth between the couple. One young mother being helped by a rural Ohio health clinic was lucky. The doctors and nurses taking care of her found out well before her baby was born that she had a *Trichomonas* infection. They also found out she had never told the baby's father about the disease.

"We asked her if she told him, and she said 'Yes,'" stated a nurse at the clinic. "But she never did tell him. We told him, and then they had a big fight about it right there."[18]

It might have been a nasty argument, but it did help the family in the end. The baby's father was able to get treated, too, preventing the mother from being reinfected.

Screening Programs

Along with partner notification, screening programs are important in preventing the spread of sexually transmitted diseases. One of the most important screening programs is the Gonococcal Isolate Surveillance Project (GISP). GISP alerts government health workers whenever more resistant strains of gonorrhea are found. The government knows the number of cases is increasing because of the testing done under the GISP program. Both public health and military STD clinics are part of the program.[19]

Donated blood is also screened for the presence of syphilis and the viruses that cause AIDS and hepatitis. Each year about 4 million patients receive blood transfusions. Until these new tests came along, donated blood and its products caused thousands of cases of AIDS.

Public health workers have also tried to detect cases of STDs before they produce symptoms, as well as cases of STDs

These Methods Do Not Prevent STDs![20]

There are many misconceptions about the best way to prevent STDs. Birth control pills are very effective at preventing pregnancy, but they offer no protection against STDs. Withdrawing the penis before ejaculation does very little to help prevent STDs. Washing or urinating right after sex does not help either.

One of the most common mistakes people make is thinking that having a steady boyfriend or girlfriend is enough protection. Carrie found out the hard way when she contracted chlamydia. Her current boyfriend had had other sex partners before her. Even though they were dating steadily at the time, his past sex life came back to haunt her.

Dr. A. Eugene Washington calls this trend "serial monogamy," one steady partner after another. He also calls it pure foolishness. "Serial monogamy is not protective! That's one of the most significant risks. They don't think of themselves at risk, but over time, they [will] have had sex with a number of different partners."[21]

Until recently, doctors believed that circumcision (removing the foreskin from the tip of the penis) could help prevent the spread of sexually transmitted diseases. However, circumcision has no effect in preventing STDs.

that do not produce noticeable symptoms. Infected people can then be treated earlier, preventing more serious complications and preventing the disease from spreading. Chlamydia rates in Alaska, Idaho, Oregon, and the state of Washington have been dropping steadily since widespread screening began in 1988. Similar projects are underway in San Francisco and Columbus, Ohio. Experts believe screening programs like these can cut the number of cases of pelvic inflammatory disease by as much as 60 percent.[22]

Preventing AIDS by Treating STDs

It is becoming clearer that preventing STDs prevents the spread of HIV. Researchers in North Carolina discovered that men infected with both HIV and another sexually transmitted disease produce semen with much higher levels of HIV than men infected with HIV alone. The HIV levels can be up to ten times higher, which means there is a much greater chance that HIV will spread.[23]

In the Privacy of Your Home

People who are too afraid to go to the doctor or a health clinic can now test themselves for HIV at home. The Food and Drug Administration has approved a home testing kit that does not require any medical training to use. A person provides a small sample of blood, then ships the test to a laboratory, where the testing is finished. After a few days, the person can call a special phone number and punch in a code to get the results. The test is completely private and confidential, although the testing company does provide information about counseling and medical referrals.

More than 60 percent of Americans at risk for contracting HIV have not been tested, according to estimates by the Centers for Disease Control and Prevention. "Too many Americans do not know their HIV status. Knowledge is power, and power leads to prevention," said Health and Human Services Secretary Donna Shalala on the day the new test was approved.[24] Two companies began selling the home test kits when they were first approved, but one company stopped selling them the very next year. Company officials said not enough people were buying the kits.[25]

Protecting Babies from HIV

The United States is enjoying one of its first big victories over HIV. A nationwide effort to protect the babies of pregnant women infected with the virus is sharply reducing the number of new infections. Infection rates in newborns were cut in half in less than two years, and some experts believe the rates could drop to as low as 2 percent. "We're pretty astounded," said John Auerbach, director of the Massachusetts health department's AIDS bureau. "The lesson is that prevention works—although it's not easy and it's not cheap."[26]

Drugs that can stop HIV from making new copies of itself can prevent many newborns from becoming infected, but the mothers must be treated before the baby is born. The infections are prevented by treating the woman with the anti-HIV drug AZT during the last six months of her pregnancy, giving

AZT to the mother during labor, then treating the newborn for six weeks after birth. Without any treatment, 25 percent of newborns would catch HIV from their mothers. With treatment, only about 10 percent of these babies become infected.[27]

Women who are infected with HIV and who smoke must do one more thing to prevent the virus from being passed to their babies. They need to quit smoking. The nicotine in cigarettes weakens blood vessels and the membranes that protect a baby inside the uterus. The combination of leaky blood vessels and leaky membranes makes it more likely that a baby will be born infected with HIV.[28]

Sex Education

Some states do not allow schools to teach their students anything about condoms or birth control. Teachers must tell students that abstinence, or avoiding sex, is the only way to avoid unwanted pregnancies and sexually transmitted diseases. Teachers must also warn their students about the potential health risks of being sexually active. Most other information about sexual activity is off limits.[29]

Schools that teach more detailed sex education classes struggle to get their message across. "They're embarrassed to hear about it," says nurse Jane Vandervort, who teaches sex education classes in local schools. "The boys . . . close it out completely." Vandervort says teens have a lot to learn. "We have girls at fourteen or fifteen who had to go to cryosurgery [to treat complications of STDs]. They don't seem to realize

More than two hundred thousand True Love Waits commitment cards were placed on the National Mall at the White House during a national rally representing teenagers' pledges to sexual abstinence before marriage.

the disease is related to their sexual activity. No lightbulb goes on. There is a real knowledge gap."[30]

Nurse Kathy Sabin struggles to educate children from an Appalachian community about abstinence and safe sex. In some areas, it is not unusual for girls to get married or pregnant while they are still in high school, so there is very little community pressure to avoid sex. "The culture says the more babies you have, the more of a woman you are. Then there was a seventeen-year-old boy who was so pleased about getting a girl pregnant. It proved he was a man now. In that culture, it was okay. That's hard to break."[31]

True Love Waits is one of many programs that uses community and positive peer pressure to help teenagers remain virgins until they get married. Most of the programs operate in local churches or with the help of local church leaders. Other chapters work on college campuses. The campaign was created in 1993 by the Baptist Sunday School Board and now involves more than forty other denominations and student groups. The international organization has sponsored several large rallies, including one in Washington, D.C., where teenagers displayed two hundred thousand pledge cards from teens promising to abstain from premarital sex.[32]

9

STD Research

The problem of sexually transmitted diseases will not go away until we have better prevention, better medicines, better vaccines, and better methods to detect STDs before they spread out of control. Scientists and doctors all over the world are working on different parts of the problem, and their work extends far beyond the AIDS epidemic. "There are STDs that can kill you besides HIV," reminds Dorothy Mann of the Family Planning Council in Philadelphia, explaining the importance of research into all STDs.[1]

Building Better Antibiotics

Many researchers are looking for better antibiotics to use against bacterial STDs. Since the bacteria that cause gonorrhea are becoming resistant to many commonly used medications, researchers want to uncover new antibiotics for doctors to prescribe. A team of researchers from Stanford University in California, the University of Wisconsin, and Brown University, for example, found a clever way to produce lots of new medicines at once. Many living things, such as molds and other fungi, produce their own antibiotics. (Penicillin originally came from mold.) The researchers looked for the enzymes that different organisms use to produce antibiotics naturally. Then they made small changes in the enzyme that would normally produce erythromycin, a common antibiotic. Changing the enzyme changed the antibiotics it produced. The researchers say they should be able to make hundreds of new compounds, some of which may turn out to be effective antibiotics. Early work showed that some of those compounds do kill bacteria, but it is too early to say whether they are safe to use in humans.[2]

Keeping Our Blood Supply Safe

Tests are now available to spot syphilis, hepatitis, and HIV in donated blood, but scientists want to develop even better tests. Current tests can pick up nearly all cases of infected blood. However, if a blood donor has been newly infected, the screening tests might miss the early signs of the infection.

There are three ways to test blood for hepatitis viruses and HIV. The first test that scientists developed looks for antibodies to the virus. The test is very sensitive, but it takes about twenty-two days for the body to build up a detectable amount of antibodies. The second test looks for an antigen, a piece of the virus's outer coat. That test works within about sixteen days of an infection.[3]

The newest test, developed by Gen-Probe, Incorporated, of San Diego, is a gene probe. It looks for the virus's genetic material and works just eleven days after infection. It can detect both hepatitis C and HIV, and it works so fast that it can spot the viruses before the person develops antibodies to them. The government is currently reviewing the test.[4]

Early Chlamydia Detection

BioStar Inc., of Boulder, Colorado, is one company that has developed a faster method to detect chlamydia infections in women. Normally, cell specimens must be grown in a laboratory for seventy-two hours before an infection can be detected. The BioStar test called optical immunoassay can provide results right in the doctor's office. A specially treated, thin, silicon wafer catches tiny pieces of the chlamydia organism. When a light reflects off the wafer, the wafer changes color from gold to bluish purple if chlamydia is present. The test requires the doctor to obtain cells from the opening to the cervix for analysis.[5]

Other researchers are developing tests that search for the DNA or genetic material of the chlamydia microbe. These tests use a basic urine sample and allow for widespread screening of high-risk groups. The tests have been used in high school health clinics in Baltimore and Los Angeles, and many cases of chlamydia that were not causing any symptoms have been found. Researchers believe widespread screening will

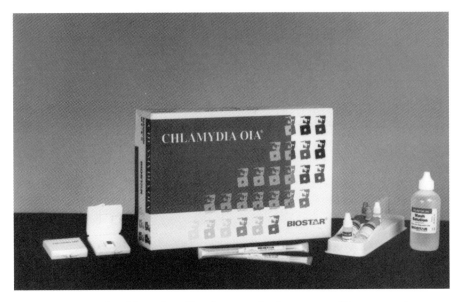

A new test for chlamydia offers faster results for women. The test can be done in a doctor's office.

make it easier to catch chlamydia before it causes serious health problems.[6]

However, DNA tests cost more than other available tests, and they require special laboratory equipment. Health workers hope to find tests that are both inexpensive and easy to run so that they can do widespread screening for both chlamydia and gonorrhea.[7]

Sugar-coated Trouble

Since spermicides prevent sexually transmitted diseases only about half the time, researchers at the University of Washington are trying to develop an ointment or gel that would stop chlamydia before it can enter cells and begin an infection. Chlamydia, although caused by bacteria, acts like a virus when it invades the body. It must get inside a person's cells to cause an infection. Researchers found out how chlamydia gets inside the cells. It uses a special chain of sugars on the outside of the bacterium to latch on to the cells it infects. The sugars fit inside molecules called receptors. If chlamydia cannot hook on to the receptor, it cannot infect the cell.

The researchers want to make molecules that look just like chlamydia's sugars. These molecules could be included in a gel or ointment, which would be spread on genital tissues. The look-alike molecules would cling to the cells that chlamydia would normally infect, preventing the chlamydia bacterium from entering the cells. Dr. Cho-chou Kuo, who is leading the team that is developing this new weapon against chlamydia, says the antibacterial gel should be inexpensive and easy to use in Third World countries, where the disease is a leading cause of blindness and infertility.[8]

A Vaccine to Fight Chlamydia

Scientists at Johns Hopkins University and the University of Massachusetts are working together on an unusual vaccine against chlamydia. It will not only immunize a person against chlamydia, but it also might help people already infected get better. "The development of this vaccine is important because people can get the disease more than once. They do not build up resistance to it as they do to many other infections," says

Judith Whittum-Hudson, associate professor of ophthalmology and researcher at the Wilmer Eye Institute at Johns Hopkins.[9]

The researchers made the vaccine by building a protein that looks like a piece of chlamydia. The real chlamydia piece is made from fat and sugar. The protein version is expected to get a much bigger response from the immune system. Therefore, the body will make many antibodies against the protein, immunizing the patient against chlamydia. The researchers have even found a way to seal the vaccine inside a capsule so that a person might be able to swallow the vaccine in pill form instead of getting a shot.

A One-Two Punch Against Hepatitis

A vaccine to protect against the hepatitis B virus has been available for many years, but it takes a series of three shots over six months to get full protection. If you want protection against other forms of hepatitis, you need to get a completely different series of shots. Researchers in Great Britain are testing a new dual-action vaccine that protects against hepatitis A and hepatitis B in just one shot.

If it gets approved, the new vaccine should help many travelers who need to go to parts of the world where hepatitis is a major problem. They can get protection against both types of hepatitis in half the normal time. Hepatitis B kills 2 million people every year and is responsible for most cases of liver cancer. In the long run, researchers hope the new vaccine will be available to people in countries with the highest rates of this deadly form of hepatitis.[10]

More Vaccines in Development

The symptoms of genital herpes are painful for most people and life-threatening for newborns. More than 30 million Americans are infected with the herpesvirus, warranting the development of a vaccine. A team of researchers at the Royal Adelaide Hospital in Australia is trying out a herpes vaccine on a small group of high-risk people. Each one has a sex partner already infected with genital herpes. The researchers hope the vaccine will protect them from catching the herpesvirus from their partners.[11]

Research groups in England and the United States are trying two different approaches to develop a vaccine against the human papillomavirus (HPV). HPV is one of the few sexually transmitted diseases that can be treated, but up to half of all HPV patients have flare-ups even after getting treated. And the longer the virus hides out in the body, the greater the chance that cervical or other genital cancers will develop. Cantab Pharmaceuticals of Cambridge, England, has a vaccine that seems to work on new HPV patients and those who suffer flare-ups. They get a series of three shots over four weeks. Dr. John St. Clair Roberts, medical director of Cantab, says none of his patients has had any flare-ups since getting the vaccine. But the first human tests were very small, and much more testing needs to be done.[12]

Researchers at the Johns Hopkins Oncology Center are still using mice to test their HPV vaccine. The vaccine is different from the British one because it targets cervical cancer cells already infected by HPV. The vaccine uses an antigen—a small piece of the human papillomavirus—to jump-start the immune system. When white blood cells detect the antigen from the vaccine, they begin looking for cells that have the same HPV antigen. When they find them, they will destroy the cells. Since only cells infected with HPV have the antigen, normal healthy cells are left alone. "The vaccine works like addressing a letter. You put the antigen in the envelope—the molecular tag—and it gets mailed to the correct address," says Dr. Drew Pardoll of Johns Hopkins.[13]

More Drugs to Fight HIV

HIV multiplies so fast it does not take long for the virus to change into a form that is resistant to the latest drug. Scientists are always looking for new ways to attack the virus.

One day, doctors might have a one-two-three punch against HIV. In addition to the reverse transcriptase (RT) inhibitors and the protease inhibitors described in Chapter 6, they hope to add a third major class of drugs: integrase inhibitors. Integrase is the enzyme that takes the DNA made by reverse transcriptase and fits it into the white blood cell's DNA. If the virus DNA does not become part of the cell, the cell will not turn into a virus factory. The virus hits a dead end.[14]

Assistant professor Pablo Tebas of the Washington University School of Medicine in St. Louis says everything researchers learn about fighting HIV can help them fight other viral diseases, too. In fact, some researchers are already using the information about protease inhibitors to develop

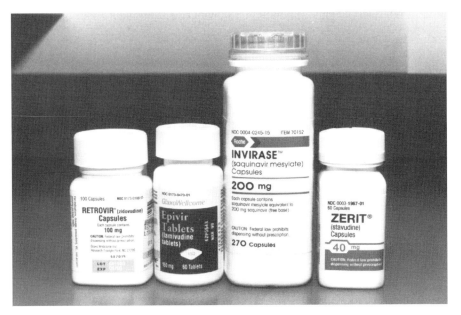

There is a growing arsenal of drugs to fight the AIDS virus.

similar drugs against a virus known as cytomegalovirus, which causes serious infections in people with compromised immune systems, such as those with AIDS.[15]

Gene Therapy for AIDS

Drugs are not the only type of therapy for AIDS patients. Researchers in California are working on gene therapy. They plan to take a gene for a key HIV protein, change it slightly, then put the gene into stem cells found in the bone marrow. Bone marrow stem cells can divide to become any kind of blood cell the body needs. With the altered gene, all new white blood cells would produce the new protein that stops HIV from reproducing. Early tests using mice were very successful. The mice essentially developed a brand-new immune system following gene therapy.[16]

Hope for an HIV Vaccine

Doctors know that no matter how many drugs are developed, there is always a chance that HIV will become resistant to them. "In the long run, it is unlikely that we will ever be able to completely eradicate HIV from somebody already infected," said Dr. Tebas of St. Louis. "Down the road, vaccines definitely are the way to go."[17]

The government agrees. President Bill Clinton challenged researchers to develop an HIV vaccine by the year 2007.[18] Congress is increasing the amount of funding for AIDS research, and Nobel Prize winner David Baltimore is now in charge of the government's efforts to develop an HIV vaccine.[19] More than two thousand volunteers have taken part in vaccine studies so far. Three new studies began in early 1998 that will involve researchers at six medical centers nationwide. Each study focuses on a different strategy to build up immunity against HIV.[20]

One of the earliest vaccines tested helps the body use two different defense systems. The first attacks free-floating HIV in the blood when a person becomes infected. The other attacks and kills cells that have been infected by HIV. The vaccine uses a harmless virus to carry tiny bits of HIV genes and a genetically engineered protein into the body. After a series of three to four shots, the vaccine improved the patients' immune responses without causing any serious side effects.[21]

However, even the most optimistic scientists do not expect to have an effective vaccine for HIV in this century. As Robert Schooley of the University of Colorado at Denver explained, "We've been working for about 100 years for a syphilis vaccine and a gonorrhea vaccine and we don't have those yet. And those are easier."[22]

Human Testing

One of the biggest problems in doing research on sexually transmitted diseases and other human illnesses is the need to do tests on humans. The horrors of the Tuskegee Study where nearly four hundred syphilis victims were left virtually untreated for forty years have had a lasting impact. Scientists must now follow very strict rules, including the rule of informed consent. Anyone who takes part in a medical study to test new drugs, vaccines, or therapies must be able to understand the possible risks of the treatment. People who take part in a study must sign a form that explains what the treatment is supposed to do and what side effects might occur during treatment.

The risks often increase when women and children take part in a medical study. This is one reason why so few medical research studies include them. Doctors are afraid that treating women might harm their reproductive systems. Even if the treatment does not hurt the woman, it might damage her baby should she become pregnant during the study. With children, it is often difficult to determine the exact risks of a treatment. Their growing bodies act differently from adults'.

Around the world, each country sets its own standards for testing new medical treatments, so a drug or vaccine that is available in one country might not be available in another. Government agencies must review all the test results before deciding whether a new treatment works and is safe enough to use. When a disease is incurable or life-threatening, like AIDS, the government tries to make it easier to get the necessary tests completed and new treatments approved.

While research continues, one thing remains clear. There are still only a few ways for sexually active teens and adults to protect themselves and others from sexually transmitted diseases: abstain from sex or use a condom, get regular physical exams, and notify all sexual partners of an STD diagnosis.

Q & A

Q: What are sexually transmitted diseases?

A: Sexually transmitted diseases, or STDs, are infections that can be passed from one person to another by sexual contact. Some STDs can also be passed from a pregnant woman to her baby, by receiving contaminated blood, or rarely, by casual contact such as sharing a towel or a toilet.

Q: What is sexual contact?

A: Sexual contact is typically vaginal intercourse where a man inserts his penis into a woman's vagina, but other types of intimate contact are also considered sexual contact. These include oral sex, anal sex, and fondling another person's genitals.

Q: What is a carrier?

A: A carrier is a person who is infected with a virus, bacterium, or other germ. They do not always show symptoms of the disease, but they can pass the disease to another person.

Q: What causes sexually transmitted diseases?

A: STDs are caused by many different germs. These can be bacteria, viruses, fungi, or protozoa. Scabies are tiny mites, and pubic lice are small insects. Scabies and pubic lice can be passed from one person to another by sexual contact, but they are not always classified as STDs.

Q: Can a person with an STD be cured?

A: Bacterial, fungal, and protozoan infections can be cured with most antibiotics. However, some bacteria are becoming resistant to common antibiotics such as penicillin and tetracycline. Many viral STDs cannot be cured. The person carries the virus for life and is sometimes killed by the virus.

Q: What does it mean to be HIV positive?

A: When a person is infected with HIV, the virus that causes AIDS, his or her blood can show signs of the infection even before any symptoms occur. At this point, the person is considered to be HIV positive. The person carries HIV in the blood and can transmit it to other people.

Q: Who is at risk of getting a sexually transmitted disease?

A: Anyone who is sexually active is at risk. Changing from vaginal to oral sex does not eliminate the risk. Teenagers are at high risk because of their high hormone levels. Women are at high risk because it is sometimes hard to notice symptoms of an infection.

Q: How can you protect yourself from becoming infected?

A: The only sure way to avoid sexually transmitted diseases is to abstain from sexual contact. Condoms for men and women provide good protection against STDs when used properly.

STDs Timeline

1492—Christopher Columbus discovered the New World.

1495—A major syphilis epidemic spread through Europe.

1530—Italian physician Girolamo Fracastoro described and named the disease syphilis.

1762—Syphilis spread north into Sweden following the Seven Years' War.

1864—The British adopted the first Contagious Disease Act, which allowed the government to imprison prostitutes found or suspected of being infected with STDs.

1879—The bacterium that causes gonorrhea was discovered.

1905—The bacterium that causes syphilis was discovered.

1909—Scientist Paul Ehrlich and his assistant developed an arsenic-based treatment for syphilis.

1912—The United States Armed Forces began distributing special kits to men in the military to protect them from sexually transmitted diseases. The ointment in the kit had to be used immediately after sexual intercourse.

1932—The United States Public Health Service began a study of untreated syphilis, using nearly four hundred black men living near Tuskegee, Alabama.

1938—The United States Syphilis Control Program began.

1943—Penicillin was developed and was originally effective in treating syphilis and gonorrhea.

1970s—The first strains of resistant gonorrhea were found.

1982—United States health officials described a new disease known as AIDS, acquired immunodeficiency syndrome.

1984—Human immunodeficiency virus, or HIV, was identified as the cause of AIDS.

1985—The first test for HIV became available.

1987—The United States Food and Drug Administration approved the drug AZT for treating HIV.

1988—Gonorrhea strains appeared that are resistant to a third group of antibiotics.

1996—Researchers found that cocktail therapy, involving multiple drugs, nearly eliminates HIV from the body.

1998—The United States Centers for Disease Control and Prevention published updated guidelines for treating and diagnosing sexually transmitted diseases.

For More Information

CDC National AIDS Hotline
(24 hours, 7 days a week)
1-800-342-2437 (English)
1-800-344-7432 (Spanish)
1-800-243-7889 (TTY for hearing impaired)

CDC National STD Hotline
Mon.-Fri. 8:00 A.M.–11:00 P.M.
1-800-227-8922

Centers for Disease Control and Prevention
1600 Clifton Road NE
Atlanta, GA 30333

Herpes Resource Center
P.O. Box 13827
Research Triangle Park, NC 27709

HIV/AIDS and TB Fax Information Service
(24 hours, 7 days a week)
1-404-332-4565

Magic Johnson Foundation
1888 Century Park East, Suite 1010
Los Angeles, CA 90067
1-310-785-0201

National AIDS Clearinghouse/Canada
1-613-725-3769

National Herpes Hotline
1-919-361-8488
9:00 A.M.–6:00 P.M. EST

Planned Parenthood
1-800-230-PLAN
(many local chapters)

True Love Waits
1-800-LUV-WAIT

Chapter Notes

Chapter 1. A Complicated Problem

1. Bradley Stoner, "Seeking Care for Sexually Transmitted Infections: Symptom Recognition, Heterodox Therapies, and 'Delay' in Biomedical Treatment," Presentation at American Anthropological Association Annual Meeting, Washington, D.C., November 15, 1995.

2. Ibid.

3. Personal interview with Bradley Stoner, M.D., assistant professor, Washington University in St. Louis, August 1997.

4. Thomas R. Eng and William T. Butler, eds., Committee on Prevention and Control of Sexually Transmitted Diseases/Institute of Medicine, *The Hidden Epidemic: Confronting Sexually Transmitted Diseases* (Washington, D.C.: National Academy Press, 1997), p. 1.

5. Laurie Garrett, "Ominous Trends on Infections," *Newsday*, May 20, 1996, p. A05.

6. Eng and Butler, p. 1.

7. Associated Press, "Still-Rampant Sexually Transmitted Diseases Called a Public Health Threat," November 19, 1996.

Chapter 2. The History of STDs

1. Geoffrey Marks and William K. Beatty, *Epidemics* (New York: Charles Scribner and Sons, 1976), p. 109.

2. Hans Konig, *Columbus: His Enterprise Exploding the Myth* (New York: Monthly Review Press, 1991), pp. 88–90.

3. Walter Libby, *The History of Medicine in Its Salient Features* (Boston: Houghton Mifflin Company, 1922), pp. 357–359.

4. "The Origin of Syphilis," *Discover*, October 24, 1996, p. 23.

5. Marks and Beatty, pp. 109–113.

6. Girolamo Fracastoro, as translated in Marks and Beatty, pp. 114, 118.

7. Ibid., p. 118.

8. Libby, pp. 357–359.

9. Marks and Beatty, pp. 113–114, 121–123.

10. Ibid., p. 113; Libby, p. 354.

11. Marks and Beatty, pp. 117–120.

12. Margaret Stacey, *The Sociology of Health and Healing* (London: Unwin Hyman Ltd., 1988), pp. 72–75.

13. Ibid., pp. 72–74.

14. Libby, p. 368.

15. Kenneth F. Kiple, *The Cambridge World History of Human Disease* (Cambridge, England: Cambridge University Press, 1993), p. 760.

16. Ibid., p. 776.

17. Ibid., p. 1053.

18. Marks and Beatty, pp. 123–124.

19. Paul Weindling, *Health, Race and German Politics Between National Unification and Nazism, 1870–1945* (Cambridge, England: Cambridge University Press, 1989), pp. 519–532.

20. Marks and Beatty, pp. 123–124.

21. WHO Office of HIV/AIDS and Sexually Transmitted Diseases, "Sexually Transmitted Diseases (STDs)—Fact Sheet," *ASD Online*, April 1996, <http://www.who.ch/programmes/asd/facsheet.htm> (February 20, 1998).

22. Edward A. Berlin, *King of Ragtime: Scott Joplin and His Era* (New York: Oxford University Press, 1994), p. 118.

23. Marks and Beatty, Illustration #6, "Representation of the *Morbus Gallicus* as Divine Punishment."

24. Henry E. Sigerist, *Civilization and Disease* (College Park, Md.: McGrath Publishing Company, 1970), p. 77.

25. Ibid., pp. 75–79.

Chapter 3. Bacterial STDs

1. Patricia Hittner, "Deadly Denial: Teenage Girls' Risk for Sexually Transmitted Disease," *Better Homes and Gardens*, vol. 72, October 1994, p. 54.

2. Ibid.

3. Thomas R. Eng and William T. Butler, eds., Committee on Prevention and Control of Sexually Transmitted Diseases/Institute of Medicine, *The Hidden Epidemic: Confronting Sexually Transmitted Diseases* (Washington, D.C.: National Academy Press, 1997), p. 1.

4. Lauran Neergaard, "Sexually Transmitted Diseases Seen as Public Health Scourge," *Associated Press*, November 19, 1996.

5. American Foundation for the Prevention of Venereal Disease, "Sexually Transmitted Disease Prevention for Everyone" pamphlet, 1988.

6. Division of STD Prevention, "Syphilis Facts," *Centers for Disease Control and Prevention*, January 23, 1998 <http://www.cdc.gov/nchstp/dstd/Syphilis_Facts.htm> (February 20, 1998).

7. WHO Office of HIV/AIDS and Sexually Transmitted Diseases, "An Overview of Selected Curable Sexually Transmitted Diseases. Figure 3," *ASD Documents*, 1996, <http://www.who.ch/programmes/asd/graphs/img004.gif> (February 20, 1998).

8. Centers for Disease Control and Prevention, "1998 Guidelines for Treatment of Sexually Transmitted Disease," *Morbidity and Mortality Weekly Report*, Vol. 47, No. RR-1, January 23, 1998, p. 69.

9. Eng and Butler, p. 31, Table 2-1.

10. Centers for Disease Control and Prevention, p. 54.

11. Personal interview with Dr. A. Eugene Washington, M.D., professor and chair of the Department of Obstetrics, Gynecology, and Reproductive Sciences at the University of California, San Francisco, January 14, 1997.

12. Ibid.

13. Jon Knowles, "Sexually Transmitted Infections: The Facts," *Planned Parenthood Federation of America, Inc.*, May 1995 <http://www.plannedparenthood.org/STI-Safesex/at-risk/default.htm> (February 23, 1998).

14. Ibid.

15. Tri D. Do, *Sexually Transmitted Diseases*, Health Promotion & Disease Prevention Project, East Boston, 1995.

Chapter 4. Viral STDs

1. Amy Linn, "Getting Hep: Hepatitis B is the Rodney Dangerfield of Diseases; It Just Can't Get Respect, But It Sure Can Kill You," *SF Weekly*, July 19, 1995.

2. Ibid.

3. "New UN World AIDS Day Report Warns that HIV Epidemic Is Far Worse than Previously Thought," *UNAIDS*, November 26, 1997, <http://www.unaids.org/highband/press/wadrelease.html> (February 20, 1998).

4. Associated Press, "Millions Commemorate World AIDS Day," December 2, 1996.

5. Ian Trontz, "Victim Bergalis Put a Face on AIDS," *Palm Beach Post*, December 8, 1996, p. 1A.

6. Sylvia Mader, *Inquiry Into Life*, 8th ed. (Dubuque: William C. Brown, 1997), pp. 408–410.

7. *Boston Globe*, "Strides Are Made in Battle Against AIDS in Infants," December 3, 1996, p. A-1.

8. Earvin "Magic" Johnson, "I'm Not Going to Stop Being Me," *Los Angeles Times*, November 3, 1996, p. C9.

9. Nancy McVicar, "Herpes Is Alive and Spreading," *Fort Lauderdale News and Sun-Sentinel*, January 3, 1992, p. E1.

10. Jane E. Brody, "Personal Health: Genital Herpes Thrives on Ignorance and Secrecy," *The New York Times*, August 12, 1992, p. C12.

11. McVicar, p. E1.

12. Cecie Starr and Beverly McMillan, eds., *Human Biology* (New York: Wadsworth Publishing Company, 1997), pp. 344–345.

13. National Cancer Institute, "Human Papillomaviruses," *Patients and Public Cancer Facts*, August 18, 1993, <http://rex.nci.nih.gov?INTRFCE_GIFS/INFO_PATS_INTR_DOC.htm> (February 20, 1998).

14. Personal interview with Jane Vandervort, Certified Nurse/Midwife, Center for Women's Health Services, Clinton Memorial Hospital, Wilmington, Ohio, January 8, 1997.

15. Arnot Ogden Medical Center, "Human Papillomavirus and Genital Warts," *Communicable Diseases Information for Patients and Public,* 1998, <http://www.aomc.org/ComDiseases/hpv.html> (February 20, 1998).

16. Judith Wasserheit et al., eds., *Research Issues in Human Behavior and Sexually Transmitted Diseases in the AIDS Era* (Washington, D.C.: American Society for Microbiology, 1991), pp. 25–26.

Chapter 5. Other STDs

1. Division of STD Prevention, "Sexually Transmitted Disease Surveillance 1995," U.S. Department of Health and Human Services, Public Health Service (Atlanta: Centers for Disease Control and Prevention, September 1996).

2. Judith Perera, "Health: Sexually Transmitted Diseases an Unnecessary Burden," *Inter Press Service,* September 29, 1995.

3. Cecie Starr and Beverly McMillan, eds., *Human Biology* (New York: Wadsworth Publishing Company, 1997), p. 346.

4. Judith Wasserheit et al., eds., *Research Issues in Human Behavior and Sexually Transmitted Diseases in the AIDS Era* (Washington, D.C.: American Society for Microbiology, 1991), p. 21.

5. Tri D. Do, Sexually Transmitted Diseases, Health Promotion & Disease Prevention Project, 1995 <http://med-www.bu.edu/people/sycamore/std/std.htm> (February 23, 1998).

Chapter 6. Treating STDs

1. Personal interview with Laura Alexoff, R.N., January 11, 1997.

2. Ibid.

3. Personal interview with Jane Vandervort, Certified Nurse/Midwife, Center for Women's Health Services, Clinton Memorial Hospital, Wilmington, Ohio, January 8, 1997.

4. Ibid.

5. Ibid.

6. Ibid.

7. Mike Toner, "Gonorrhea Still Eluding Drugs," *Atlanta Journal-Constitution*, January 20, 1996, p. G1.

8. Laboratory Centre for Disease Control, "Emergence of *Neisseria Gonorrhoeae* Strains With Decreased Susceptibility to Ciprofloxacin—Quebec, 1994–1995," *Canada Communicable Disease Report*, vol. 22-15, August 1, 1996.

9. Personal interview with Bradley Stoner, M.D., assistant professor, Washington University in St. Louis, January 1997.

10. U.S. Centers for Disease Control and Prevention, "Summary of Notifiable Diseases 1996," *Morbidity and Mortality Weekly Report*, vol. 45, no. 53, October 31, 1997.

11. Christine Gorman, "Man of the Year: The Disease Detective," *Time*, January 6, 1997, pp. 56–70.

12. Personal interview with Pablo Tebas, M.D., AIDS Clinical Trials Unit of the School of Medicine, Washington University in St. Louis, January 3, 1997.

13. Daniel Q. Haney, "Dramatic Decline in U.S. AIDS Deaths in 1997," *Associated Press*, February 3, 1998.

14. Personal interview with Pablo Tebas.

15. Anthony S. Fauci et al., "Guidelines for the Use of Antiretroviral Agents in HIV-Infected Adults and Adolescents," National Institutes of Health, November 5, 1997.

16. Reuter Information Service, "New Drugs Mean Hope for Herpes," March 17, 1997.

17. Arnot Ogden Medical Center, "Human Papillomavirus and Genital Warts," *Communicable Diseases Information for Patients and Public,* 1998, <http://www.aomc.org/ComDiseases/hpv.html> (February 20, 1998).

18. Personal interview with Kathy Sabin, R.N., January 19, 1997.

19. Ibid.

Chapter 7. STDs in Society

1. Thomas R. Eng and William T. Butler, eds., Committee on Prevention and Control of Sexually Transmitted Diseases/Institute of Medicine, *The Hidden Epidemic: Confronting Sexually Transmitted Diseases* (Washington, D.C.: National Academy Press, 1997), p. 1.

2. Monica Davey, "AIDS Can't Rob Them of Living," *St. Petersburg Times*, December 13, 1993, p. 1B.

3. Larry Tye, "Ryan White Dies from Complications of AIDS," *The Boston Globe*, April 9, 1990, p. 1.

4. Personal interview with Deborah Schoeberlein, executive director of Redefining Actions and Decisions, January 2, 1997.

5. Reuter Information Service, "New Drugs Mean Hope for Herpes," March 17, 1997.

6. James H. Jones, *Bad Blood: The Tuskegee Syphilis Experiment* (New York: The Free Press, 1993), pp. 122–128.

7. Eddie Pells, "Tuskegee Victim Tenders Forgiveness in Advance; the Nation Apologizes," *Austin-American Druggist*, vol. 213, no. 4, p. 66.

8. Jones, pp. 25–28, 219.

9. Jodi Edna, "U.S. Apologizes for Tuskegee Study," *Pittsburgh Post Gazette*, May 17, 1997, p. A1.

10. Michael Gammaitoni and Kathy Hitchens, "Preventing Sexually Transmitted Disease," *American Druggist*, vol. 213, no. 4., p. 66.

11. "New UN World AIDS Day Report Warns That HIV Epidemic Is Far Worse than Previously Thought," *UNAIDS*, November 26, 1997, <http://www.unaids.org/highband/press/wadrelease.html> (February 20, 1998).

12. Centers for Disease Control and Prevention, "Youth Risk Behavior Surveillance—United States, 1995," *Morbidity and Mortality Weekly Report*, vol. 45, no. SS-4, September 27, 1996.

13. Margaret Stacey, *The Sociology of Health and Healing* (London: Unwin Hyman Ltd., 1988), p. 75.

14. Personal interview with Dr. A. Eugene Washington, M.D., professor and chair of the Department of Obstetrics, Gynecology, and Reproductive Sciences at the University of California, San Francisco, January 14, 1997.

15. National Center for HIV, STD, & TB Prevention, "The Challenge of STD Prevention in the United States," *Division of STD Prevention*, November 1996, <http://www.cdc.gov/nchstp/dstd/STD_Prevention_in_the_United_States.htm> (February 20, 1998).

16. Ibid.

17. Jacques Boyer, "Infectious Disease War Goes On Despite Battles Won: WHO," *Agence-France-Presse*, April 7, 1997.

18. Eng and Butler, pp. 76–77.

19. Personal interview with Washington.

20. Philip Elmer-Dewitt, "Man of the Year: Turning the Tide," *Time*, January 6, 1997, pp. 54–55.

21. Pascal Zerling, "Trial of 'HIV Positive Don Juan' Sparks Finnish AIDS Debate," *Agence-France-Presse*, January 28, 1997.

22. Scott Winokur, "New Wave of Litigation Expands Women's Rights to the Bedroom," *The San Francisco Examiner*, January 28, 1996, p. A1.

23. Ibid.

Chapter 8. Preventing STDs

1. Shari Roan, "America's Silent Epidemic," *Los Angeles Times*, October 26, 1994, p. A1.

2. William T. Butler, "Prepared Remarks," Committee on Prevention and Control of Sexually Transmitted Diseases, Institute of Medicine, November 19, 1996.

3. Anton Ferreira, "Worst-hit Africa Gives Little Thought to AIDS Day," *Reuters North American Wire*, December 1, 1996.

4. Personal interview with Bradley Stoner, M.D., assistant professor, Washington State University in St. Louis, January 1997.

5. JAMA HIV/AIDS Information Center, "Do Condoms Work?" *Center for AIDS Prevention Studies, University of California, San Francisco*, February 1995, <http://www.ama-assn.org/special/hiv/preventn/ prevent2.htm> (February 20, 1998).

6. Centers for Disease Control and Prevention, "Facts About Condoms and Their Use in Preventing HIV Infection and Other STDs" pamphlet, February 1996.

7. Michael Gammaitoni and Kathy Hitchens, "Preventing Sexually Transmitted Disease," *American Druggist*, vol. 213, no. 4., p. 66.

8. Charles Henderson, "Contraception (Female Condom) Importance Acknowledged in HIV Prevention," *AIDS Weekly Plus*, December 9, 1996.

9. Charles Henderson, "International (Africa) Zimbabwe Women Petition State on Female Condom," *AIDS Weekly Plus*, December 23, 1996.

10. Roper Starch Worldwide, Inc., "Latest Opinions," *The Public Pulse*, vol. 11, no. 8, August 1996, p. 7.

11. Nancy Sheehan, "Wachusett Condom Issue Back," *Telegram & Gazette*, October 2, 1996, p. B6.

12. Centers for Disease Control and Prevention, "Youth Risk Behavior Surveillance—United States, 1995," *Morbidity and Mortality Weekly Report*, vol. 45, no. SS-4, September 27, 1996.

13. D. A. Cohen, "How To Implement a Community-Based Condom Accessibility Program," presentation at National STD Prevention Conference, December 1996.

14. Thomas R. Eng and William T. Butler, eds., Committee on Prevention and Control of Sexually Transmitted Diseases/Institute of Medicine, *The Hidden Epidemic: Confronting Sexually Transmitted Diseases* (Washington, D.C.: National Academy Press, 1997), p. 126

15. Personal interview with Dorothy Mann, executive director of the Family Planning Council of Philadelphia, January 17, 1997.

16. B. Krekeler et al., "Hepatitis B Vaccine Series Completion by High-Risk Adolescents Receiving STD Services," presentation at National STD Prevention Conference, December 1996.

17. Susan Okie, "Hepatitis B Vaccine May Block Liver Cancer," *Washington Post*, July 1, 1997, p. 21.

18. Personal interview with Jane Vandervort, Certified Nurse/Midwife, Center for Women's Health Services, Clinton Memorial Hospital, Wilmington, Ohio, January 8, 1997.

19. K. K. Fox, "The Gonococcal Isolate Surveillance Project: Sentinel Surveillance for Antimicrobial Resistance," presentation at National STD Prevention Conference, December 1996.

20. Ferreira; Roan, p. A1; David Perlman, "Study Finds Circumcised Men More Sexually Adventurous But Procedure Has No Health Benefits," *San Francisco Chronicle*, April 2, 1997, p. A4.

21. Personal interview with Dr. A. Eugene Washington, M.D., professor and chair of the Department of Obstetrics, Gynecology, and Reproductive Sciences at the University of California, San Francisco, January 14, 1997.

22. Division of STD Prevention, *Sexually Transmitted Disease Surveillance*, 1995, U.S. Centers for Disease Control and Prevention, Atlanta, September 1996.

23. David Williamson, "New Study Proves Treating STDs Reduces Infectiousness of HIV," *University of North Carolina-Chapel Hill News Service*, June 27, 1997.

24. Donna Shalala, "Prepared Remarks," secretary, Department of Health and Human Services, May 14, 1996.

25. *The New York Times* News Service, "Federal Warnings Preceded Withdrawal of Home HIV Test from Market," July 3, 1997.

26. *Boston Globe*, "Strides Are Made in Battle Against AIDS in Infants," December 3, 1996.

27. Regina McEnery, "Drugs Shield Fetuses From Mom's HIV," *Asbury Park Press*, July 12, 1996, p. A1.

28. Reuter Information Service, "Maternal Smoking Increases HIV Risk in Fetus," April 1, 1997.

29. John Newsom, "Students Advised to Abstain," *News & Record*, July 20, 1996, p. BH2.

30. Personal interview with Jane Vandervort.

31. Personal interview with Kathy Sabin, R.N., January 17, 1997.

32. Baptist Sunday School Board, "Mission Statement," True Love Waits, Nashville, 1996.

Chapter 9. STD Research

1. Personal interview with Dorothy Mann, executive director of the Family Planning Council of Philadelphia, January 17, 1997.

2. David Salisbury, "New Approach for Producing Novel Antibiotics Demonstrated," Stanford University News Release, July 17, 1997, <http://www.eurekalert.org/releases/Stanford-antibiotics.html> (February 20, 1998).

3. Jane Allen, "New Blood Test Could Halve Transfusions Tainted by AIDS and Hepatitis," *Associated Press*, December 10, 1996.

4. Ibid.

5. BioStar Inc., "Chlamydia OAI: An Enhanced Optical Immunoassay for the Rapid Detection of Chlamydia Antigen from EndoCervical Swabs" pamphlet, November 27, 1995, pp. 1–2.

6. C. A. Gaydos et al., "Urine Screening for Chlamydia Trachomatis in High School Teens by Polymerase Chain Reaction (PCR) and Ligase Chain Reaction (LCR)," presentation at National STD Prevention Conference, December 1996; I. E. Dyer et al., "Chlamydia Screening in Los Angeles County High School Students by Using a Urine Ligase Chain Reaction Assay," presentation at National STD Prevention Conference, December 1996.

7. C. M. Clark et al., "DNA Amplification Tests for Chlamydia Screening—Practicalities of Implementation—Experiences from the Field," presentation at National STD Prevention Conference, December 1996.

8. Julie Rathbun, "UW Research May Lead to Contraceptive Gel to Prevent Chlamydia, the Most Prevalent Sexually Transmitted Disease," University of Washington news release, December 18, 1996.

9. Marc Kusinitz, "Vaccine May Protect Against Major Cause of Blindness," Office of Communications and Public Affairs, Johns Hopkins Medical Institutions, October 15, 1996.

10. Reuter Information Service, "Britain Launches a New Vaccine for Hepatitis," January 15, 1997.

11. South Australian Health Commission, "Genital Herpes Vaccine Trials," December 17, 1997, <http://www.stdservices.on.net/news/archive/hsfv_vax/hsv-vax.htm> (February 23, 1998).

12. Steven Thompson, "Phase I and IIa Safety and Immunogenecity of TA-GW, a Recombinant Vaccine for the Treatment of Genital Warts," 15th International Papillomavirus Workshop, Brisbane, Australia, December 29, 1996.

13. Karin Twilde, "Hopkins Researchers Develop Genetically Engineered Cervical Cancer Vaccine," Office of Public Affairs, Johns Hopkins Medical Institutions, January 1, 1996.

14. Geoffrey Cowley, "Targeting a Deadly Scrap of Genetic Code," *Newsweek*, December 2, 1996, pp. 68–69.

15. Personal interview with Pablo Tebas, M.D., AIDS Clinical Trials Unit of the School of Medicine, Washington University in St. Louis, January 3, 1997.

16. David Perlman, "FDA Approves Anti-HIV Gene Testing: Therapy Trials to Be Used to Bolster Immune Systems," *San Francisco Chronicle*, December 18, 1996, p. A2.

17. Personal interview with Tebas.

18. Gene Gibbons, "Clinton Sets Goal to Develop AIDS Vaccine by 2007," Reuter Information Service, May 19, 1997.

19. Christine Gorman, "Man of the Year: The Disease Detective," *Time*, January 6, 1997, pp. 56–70.

20. Laurie K. Doepel, "Novel Concepts Put to the Test in Three New AIDS Vaccine Trials," NIAID *News Office of Communications*, January 14, 1998, <http://www.niaid.nih.gov/newsroom/aveg.htm> (February 20, 1998).

21. Lisa Krieger, "Two-Pronged AIDS Vaccine Developed," *The San Francisco Examiner*, January 27, 1997, p. A3.

22. Wire Service Reports, "AIDS Fighters Hopeful," *The News and Observer*, January 26, 1997.

Glossary

abstinence—Not taking part in. For example, sexual abstinence is not taking part in sexual activity.

anal—Referring to the anus.

antibiotics—Medicines that are able to kill bacteria, fungi, and protozoa. Antibiotics cannot kill viruses.

antibodies—Small proteins produced by the body to protect against invaders such as microbes.

antigen—A small piece of protein or sugar that is recognized by an antibody as foreign, stimulating the antibody to fight it.

anus—The opening to the rectum; the feces empty out of the rectum by passing through the anus.

cervical—Referring to the cervix.

cervix—The narrow, necklike opening to the uterus.

condom—A thin protective covering to prevent sperm from entering the vagina and to protect against the spread of sexually transmitted diseases. Latex condoms help prevent HIV infection. A male condom is worn over the penis. A female condom fits inside the vagina.

cryosurgery—An operation using extreme cold to freeze tissue damaged by disease.

douche—A rinse or wash used to clear out secretions inside the vagina.

ectopic pregnancy—Any pregnancy that occurs outside the uterus. Since most ectopic pregnancies occur in the fallopian tubes, they are often referred to as tubal pregnancies.

ejaculation—The muscular contractions that quickly move sperm and semen out of the penis.

epidemic—A disease affecting a very large number of people at one time.

fallopian tubes—Narrow tubes that connect a woman's ovaries and uterus. The fallopian tubes provide a pathway for eggs.

genitals—The external sex organs of a male or female.

heterosexual—Involving people of two different sexes.

homosexual—Involving people of only one sex.

immune deficiency—A disease or disorder that makes it difficult for the body to fight infections.

immunoassay—A test that uses antibodies to detect very tiny quantities of a substance or microbe.

infectious—Able to infect others; able to spread a disease.

infertile—Unable to produce offspring.

intercourse—Sexual activity involving the insertion of a man's penis into a woman's vagina.

lymph glands—Small structures located in various parts of the body where many white blood cells are produced and stored.

monogamy—The practice of having a single mate during a period of time.

pelvic inflammatory disease—A sometimes fatal infection involving the upper reproductive tract of a woman.

penis—The male reproductive organ used to transport semen.

puberty—The developmental years when a child becomes sexually mature.

quarantine—Sealing off an area to prevent the spread of a disease.

reproductive tract—All of the organs and structures involved in reproduction.

semen—A whitish liquid containing fluid and sperm. Ejaculation during sexual intercourse sends semen through the penis into a woman's vagina.

spermicide—An ointment or gel that is able to kill sperm.

surveillance—Keeping a watch or lookout. Medical surveillance involves watching for outbreaks of disease or monitoring the spread of disease.

transfusion—Providing blood to a person in need, such as an accident victim or a surgery patient.

urethra—The canal that carries urine out of the body. In males, the urethra also carries semen during ejaculation.

uterus—Also known as the womb. A small, pear-shaped organ in a female where a fertilized egg grows into a baby. The outside consists of strong muscles, which contract during labor.

vaccine—A medication that prevents the development of a disease by causing the body to produce antibodies against a particular microbe.

vagina—The pathway between the outside of the body and the cervix. A baby passes through the vagina during a normal birth; the penis is inserted into the vagina during sexual intercourse.

Further Reading

Books and Reports

Committee on Prevention and Control of Sexually Transmitted Diseases/Institute of Medicine. *The Hidden Epidemic: Confronting Sexually Transmitted Diseases.* Washington, D.C.: National Academy Press, 1996.

Division of STD Prevention. *Sexually Transmitted Disease Surveillance, 1995.* Atlanta: U.S. Centers for Disease Control and Prevention, 1996.

Jones, James H. *Bad Blood: The Tuskegee Syphilis Experiment.* New York: The Free Press, 1993.

Konig, Hans. *Columbus: His Enterprise Exploding the Myth.* New York: Monthly Review Press, 1991.

Majure, Janet. *AIDS.* Springfield, N.J.: Enslow Publishers, Inc., 1998.

Marks, Geoffrey, and William K. Beatty. *Epidemics.* New York: Charles Scribner and Sons, 1976.

Nourse, Alan E. *Sexually Transmitted Diseases.* New York: Franklin Watts, Inc., 1992.

Pamphlets

Sexually Transmitted Disease Prevention For Everyone. American Foundation for the Prevention of Venereal Disease, 1988 (Pub. code 0629).

Sexually Transmitted Diseases. Health Promotion & Disease Prevention Project. East Boston, 1995.

Sexually Transmitted Infections: The Facts. Planned Parenthood Federation of America, Inc., May 1995.

Articles

Associated Press. "Still-Rampant Sexually Transmitted Diseases Called a Public Health Threat." November 19, 1996.

Associated Press. "Millions Commemorate World AIDS Day." December 2, 1996.

Brody, Jane E. "Personal Health: Genital Herpes Thrives on Ignorance and Secrecy." *The New York Times*, August 12, 1992, p. C12.

Davey, Monica. "AIDS Can't Rob Them of Living." *St. Petersburg Times*, December 13, 1993, p. 1B.

Gammaitoni, Michelle, and Kathy Hitchens. "Preventing Sexually Transmitted Disease." *American Druggist*, vol. 213, no. 4., p. 66.

Henderson, Charles. "Contraception (Female Condom) Importance Acknowledged in HIV Prevention." *AIDS Weekly Plus*, December 9, 1996.

Hittner, Patricia. "Deadly Denial: Teenage Girls' Risk for Sexually Transmitted Disease." *Better Homes and Gardens*, vol. 72, October 1994, p. 54.

Johnson, Earvin. "I'm Not Going to Stop Being Me." *Los Angeles Times*, November 3, 1996, p. C-9.

Kirby, Douglas, and Nancy Brown. "Condom Availability Programs in U.S. Schools." *Family Planning Perspectives*, vol. 28, no. 5, September–October 1996.

Krieger, Lisa. "Two-Pronged AIDS Vaccine Developed." *The San Francisco Examiner*, January 27, 1997, p. A3.

Leland, John. "The End of AIDS?" *Newsweek*, December 2, 1996, pp. 64–74.

Lowe, Denis S. "Stop HIV Spread Among Kids." *Cincinnati Enquirer*, June 21, 1996, p. A-19.

Newsom, John. "Students Advised To Abstain." *News & Record*, July 20, 1996, p. BH2.

"The Origin of Syphilis." *Discover Magazine*. October 24, 1996, p. 23.

Perlman, David. "AIDS Continues Deadly March Around the World." *San Francisco Chronicle*, November 28, 1996, p. A-1.

Roper Starch Worldwide, Inc. "Latest Opinions." *The Public Pulse*, vol. 11, no. 8, August, 1996, p. 7.

"Some Hope on Third-World AIDS." *The New York Times*. October 7, 1996, p. A-16.

"Strides Are Made in Battle Against AIDS in Infants." *Boston Globe*. December 3, 1996.

Twilde, Karin. "Hopkins Researchers Develop Genetically Engineered Cervical Cancer Vaccine." Johns Hopkins Medical Institutions Office of Public Affairs, January 1, 1996.

Tye, Larry. "Ryan White Dies from Complications of AIDS." *The Boston Globe*, April 9, 1990, p. 1.

Wire Service Reports. "AIDS Fighters Hopeful." *The News and Observer*, January 26, 1997.

Internet Resources

American Medical Association. HIV/AIDS Information Center. 1998.
<http://www.ama-assn.org/special/hiv/> (February 26, 1998).

The Board of Trustees of the University of Illinois. "Sexually Transmitted Diseases." *McKinley Health Center.* May 26, 1996. <http://www.uiuc.edu/departments/mckinley/health-info/sexual/stds/Stds.html> (February 26, 1998).

CDC National Center for HIV, STD & TB Prevention. *Division of STD Prevention.* February 20, 1998. <http://www.cdc.gov/nchstp/dstd/dstdp.html> (February 26, 1998).

CDC. *National AIDS Clearinghouse.* n.d. <http://www.cdcnac.org> (February 26, 1998).

Northwestern University Health Service. *Sexuality and Related Topics.* February 24, 1997. <http://www.nwu.edu/health/sexuality.html> (February 26, 1998).

Planned Parenthood Federation of America. *Planned Parenthood.* 1998. <http://www.plannedparenthood.org> (February 26, 1998).

U.S. Department of Health & Human Services. *CDC National Center for Health Statistics.* January 2, 1998. <http://www.cdc.gov/nchswww/> (February 26, 1998).

WHO Office of HIV/AIDS and STDs. "STDs Fact Sheet." *ASD Online.* April 1996. <http://www.who.ch/programmes/asd/facsheet.htm> (February 26, 1998).

Index